W9-AVJ-151

Discovering Matthew

by Jim Wilcox

EDITOR
David Caudle

EDITORIAL ASSISTANT
Edie Nash

EXECUTIVE EDITOR
Rick Edwards

Copyright 1996
Beacon Hill Press of Kansas City
ISBN 083-411-5743

All Scripture quotations, unless otherwise indicated, are from the *Holy Bible, New International Version*® (NIV®). Copyright © 1973, 1978, 1984 by International Bible Society. Used by permission of Zondervan Publishing House. All rights reserved.

Scripture from *The Message* (TM). Copyright © 1993. Used by permission of NavPress Publishing Group.

Contents

Introduction

This study book has been created with the prayer that the Word of God will find a place in your heart and mind so that you will be equipped to be an effective disciple of Jesus Christ.

If you are using this study book as a part of a Bible study group, then you are using it to its best benefit. In your group you will learn to trust each other as you discover Matthew and share truths that will help you learn from each other. There is a personal time of discovery to complement each group session, which will lead you into greater insights. *Discovering Matthew* is both an excellent group workbook and a personal workbook.

If you do not have a group to study with, you can still gain great benefit from using all the studies on your own. Simply adapt the group questions when needed.

If you are using this study book as a part of a Bible quizzing program, you will be getting the full benefit out of quizzing by doing so. But be careful! The temptation to slack off on your discovery workbook when you prepare for tournaments will come at one time or another. Don't give in to that temptation! Gain the full benefit of memory work and application of biblical principles to your life as a disciple of Jesus Christ.

You are now invited to begin this special journey through Matthew with Personal Discovery No. 1. Before you begin, pause for a moment of prayer, asking God to bless the time you give to the study of His Word and to give you the desire to grow in your relationship with Him. And be prepared to make some exciting changes in your life!

SPECIAL INSTRUCTIONS: Each Personal Discovery is divided into specific sections. All of them can be done at once, but it will be more manageable—and probably more meaningful—if you do just one per day. In this way, the Personal Discoveries can be used as guides for your personal devotional times, as well as preparation for the Discovery Group sessions.

1

This Changes Everything

STUDY SCRIPTURE: Matthew 1:1—4:11

KEY VERSE: "And a voice from heaven said, 'This is my Son, whom I love; with him I am well pleased'" (Matthew 3:17).

PERSONAL DISCOVERY

1. WELCOME TO MATTHEW

Most people can look back at their lives and see stages or divisions, what Gail Sheehy calls "passages." These are particular accomplishments or setbacks, birthdays or graduations, relocations or changes in careers that alter the direction of our lives so greatly that we remember them forever. Even at your age, you can probably mark several of these evolutionary and revolutionary occasions: starting kindergarten, becoming a Christian, moving from one city to another, your first kiss, your first date, graduating from junior high, and heading into high school. Your parents have survived those same moments too . . . and then some (not the least of which was your birth).

Humanity itself also has experienced its own set of "passages." The Bible recounts the first man and woman, Adam and Eve; the great flood; the Roman Empire. American history books recount the discovery of the New World; the American Revolution, the Civil War, the Great Depression, two world wars; the first landing on the moon. But there is one single event, one shining moment, that divides the calendar of humankind like no other—the birth, life, death, and resurrection of Jesus of Nazareth, the Messiah, the Promised Man. No other incident in the past or future can separate the ages like Jesus' coming.

His birth marks the beginning of the new covenant, the contractual addendum that fulfills our relationship with the Creator of the universe. Jesus' life shows us mortals what the immortal God is really like. Jesus' death affirms the Father's sense of self-giving love. And His resurrection marks the beginning of His life-giving "forever presence," in the person of the Holy Spirit.

It changed everything.

The Book of Matthew is not only the first book of the New Testament (duh!) but also the first of what are called the Synoptic Gospels, along with the Books of Mark and Luke. If you remember your Latin from elementary school (and who doesn't?), you know that *synoptic* comes from two words: *syn* meaning "same" and *optic* meaning "see" or "witness." The word *gospel*, of course, translates into "good news," so the "Synoptic Gospels" literally means "Corresponding Accounts of the Good News." This corroboration offers even the most skeptical of readers a sense of authenticity and confirmation. (John's language, style, order, and observations are quite different from his three contemporaries, so his Gospel is not included under this umbrella term.)

As you know, there are three basic genres or types of writing in the New Testament (hereafter referred to as the new covenant): there are the books, the letters, and the prophecies. The Book of Matthew is a story, more particularly a theological biography, of the life, activities, thoughts, and frustrations of Jesus, the Son of God. It fits the classical characteristics of good narrative writing, and even though it is nonfiction, it contains great fictional technique—like a great novel. It has a beginning with setting and main character, a chronicle of conflicts that reach a peak or climax, then a resolution (what literary experts call the denouement) that concludes the story. It's simply fascinating reading.

Matthew, as you may know, was one of the 12 disciples (or apostles) who lived with Jesus during His ministry on earth. Unlike many of the chosen dozen, however, Matthew had led a life completely unworthy of the calling. He had been a tax collector, not the noblest of career choices back then, and a dirty scoundrel as well, cheating many people out of their hard-earned incomes. It seems significant, then, that the new covenant that God initiates with humanity begins with the account written by Matthew, a man whose own destiny was transformed through the saving grace of Jesus Christ.

This Gospel was written between A.D. 60 and 80, but most scholars place it early in that time frame. Its original language was Greek, so obviously it was written for Greek-speaking Jews, and it contains more references to the Old Testament than any other new covenant writer, in order to show that Jesus is the fulfillment of the Jewish messianic prophecy and hope. It is organized around Jesus' five great discourses, or speeches, with narrative elements providing transition between each.

Before we begin our study of Matthew's Gospel, chapter by chapter, verse by verse, you ought to take an hour or so to review this familiar story by skimming and scanning the main sections. When you get to a favorite passage, read it carefully again. Try to picture the faces of those in that episode. How were they dressed? What had their day been like up to that point? What kinds of foods did they eat? How did they wear their hair or walk along the dusty paths? What sounds do you hear? Can you smell the marketplaces or the homes? Enter into the scene fully.

After this overview, complete the following statements:

- The fact that Jesus was a human being means

- The fact that Jesus was God means

- One story from Matthew's book that strikes me is

- If I could sit down with Jesus right now, I would ask Him

- If I had to capture this book in one sentence, it would be

2. OVERVIEW

This first section of Matthew will seem like old stuff to you, perhaps, for it is told and retold many times throughout the Christian year, particularly at Christmas. Prior to your study, however, it would be good for you to read it as if you had never seen it or heard about it before. It's a fairly big chunk, so give yourself 30 minutes or so. Then answer the following questions:

- What seems to be the key element to Matthew's account of Christ's birth and infancy?

- Is there anything mentioned that you either did not know or had forgotten?

- Why is John the Baptist so important to the story?

- If you had been Jesus' parents, what might you have done differently?

3. ROOTS ON THE FAMILY TREE (1:1-25)

Whew! Forty-two generations! That may seem like just a bunch of biblical trivia to you, but to Matthew it was a strong message that Jesus was the fulfillment of centuries-old prophecy. And he used it to establish Jesus as the Messiah to his Jewish audience.

Remember that Sarah, the wife of Abraham (who begins the list of ancestors in verse 2), was barren, so it was only God's divine intervention that enabled them to produce what was to become "God's people." This reminder to Matthew's readers of their origins set the stage for his description of the conception of Jesus, which was similarly miraculous but even more dramatic. This recitation of lineage is then followed by the actual birth of the baby Jesus, which changed the world forever.

When you have finished reading the first chapter of Matthew, answer these questions:

- Note that Matthew divides the genealogy into three sections. What do you think was his purpose? What do you notice about each division?

- Choose one name from each section and write down all you know or can find out about that person.

  1.

  2.

  3.

- Joseph was tempted to divorce Mary when he found out about her pregnancy. What do you suppose was going through his mind?

- If you had been in Joseph's shoes, what would that dream (vv. 20-21) have done to you?

- Look up the name Jesus in the biggest and best dictionary you can find and discover its meaning. Write it down here and think about it.

4. JOY TO THE WORLD (2:1-23)

No birth in the history of humanity has been celebrated as widely, eagerly, or religiously as the birth of this little Baby. After you read this particular account, respond to the following questions and instructions:

- What makes the birth of Jesus similar to what you know about your own birth?

- If you had been Mary's mother or father, what advice might you have offered her before she left for Egypt?

- Write down three things Mary and Joseph did that you think were good decisions.

- Just what exactly is Herod's problem? Why is this birth so important to him?

- There are several dreams and angel messages in this passage. Write them down and jot down your opinion as to what purpose each serves.

5. THE WANDER YEARS (3:1—4:11)

Jesus' childhood is pretty much left out of Scripture. Oh, there's Luke's story of the visit to the Temple and His parents' subsequent panic, and there's a little bit about Joseph's carpentry business, but for the most part we jump from Jesus the baby to Jesus the man. This section of Matthew shows God's plan for Jesus, through the parallel life of John the Baptist. After you finish reading this chapter and a half, answer the following items:

- The Baptist held no punches when he preached. We have only one of his sermons in Scripture, but from it we can see he was a strong orator with even stronger opinions. What was his message in verses 7-12?

- Enter the Nazarene. Jesus comes to the river to be baptized. Describe that scene in your own words.

- What is John's reaction to Jesus' request? Does that seem fitting or out of place? Why?

- Describe the appearance of John the Baptist. Use all five of your senses.

- Why was God pleased with Jesus at this point? What had He done?

- Jesus immediately goes off by himself to meditate and is tempted. List the three temptations and Jesus' response to each. What does this tell you about the character of Christ?

DISCOVERY GROUP

STUDY SCRIPTURE: Matthew 1:1—4:11

KEY VERSE: Matthew 3:17

It's a Boy!

Your study group is throwing (don't you love that term?) a baby shower for Mary and Joseph. As a host or hostess, your job is to register each guest's name and the gift he or she brought to the Baby so that the parents can send appropriate Thank-you cards. You know what the three Magi brought, but the other folks and their gifts will have to be products of your imagination. You might want to do this on your own at first, then as a group.

Date and time:

Location:

Hosts/hostesses:

Guest   *Gift*

A Baby Book

One of the more thoughtful gifts from the shower is a baby book—a record of the infant's birth and first years. With the help of a healthy and creative mind—or a friend who has one—fill out the information so that Mary and Joseph can remember these formative years.

First signs that we were "expecting":

Trip to the birthing place:

We named the baby:
Arrival time:
Date:

Color of hair:
Height:
Weight:
Peculiarities:

Parents' first impressions and reactions:

Comments of friends and relatives:

Current news headlines:

Political figures:

Fashions, fads, etc.:

Best-selling books:

Age when He first slept through the night:
Age when He crawled:
Age when He walked:
Favorite foods:

Favorite people:

Favorite outfit:
Baby's name for Mother:
Baby's name for Father:
First words:
Baby's first doctor visit, and doctor's instructions:

Baby's favorite activities at:
    1 year old—
    5 years old—
    10 years old—
    15 years old—
Baby's first Christmas:

Baby's early travels:

Yield Not

You've sneaked into the fourth meeting of the local chapter of Temptations Anonymous, a growing group of people you know who are trying desperately to break their bad habits. As you listen to them introduce themselves, see if you can come up with some sound advice for them.

"Hi, my name is **Molly Mallhopper,** and I'm a shopaholic."

"Hi, Molly!" everybody said in unison.

"I've not been to a shoppin' mall in six weeks, but I'm havin' an awful time, y'all. I really miss walkin' around and buyin' all the great stuff I see: the shoes, the jackets, the jeans, but most of all the jewelry. I really love earrings and bracelets, y'all, I really do. I have 76 pairs of earrings at home and 10 more in my car. I haven't counted all my bracelets, but I'm on my second rack. I know it got outta hand with my mom's credit card, but that was the only 'bad' thing I did, y'all, and I really miss everybody comin' over to me at school on Monday to see the new stuff I bought over the weekend. I really do."

No sooner had Molly sat down than the next person stood up.

"Hi, my name is **Freddy Fastlane,** and I'm a speedaholic."

"Hi, Freddy!"

"I've had this cool truck since I was a junior, man, and I don't want to brag or anything, but it can flat-out romp. I used to get it up to 60 on my street without even flipping out of third gear. And I live on the corner, man. I only had four wrecks last year, and a couple of them were not my fault. Those old people just don't know when to stay at home, that's all. And if that cop hadn't moved in on my street, I'd still be haulin' doughnuts. But the dude slapped me with eight tickets, and here I sit. My dad had to bring me here tonight. If only I had learned not to get caught—I'd still be 'The Bullet.'"

You thought you'd heard it all, but then *she* stood up. All 5 feet 10, blond, voluptuous inches of her. She had legs from here to New York City and curves in places where most cover girls don't even have places. Her eyes seemed to be filled with Caribbean island seas, and her smile outshone the sun *and* the moon. To put it in a word, "Gagah."

"Hi," she moaned, "my name is **Vixen** and I'm a manaholic."

"Hi, Vixen!"

"I've never been lonely, you know, and I don't ever want to be. Well, who ever wants to be lonely, you know? But a few months ago I started to realize that, even with all my friends hanging around all the time, I didn't know sometimes who that person was in my mirror, looking back at me. Oh, this is hard to say out loud. I have been able to attract every man I've ever wanted, and I know all the tricks it takes to get the kind of things I want from them, whether it's cars, luxurious vacations, or diamond necklaces. (That got Molly's attention.) It also scares me about all these diseases I keep hearing about, so I've sworn off the sex and the games, but it's been hard, you know. Sometimes at night I cry myself to sleep, and I think about going back to the old life, 'cause I miss the attention I used to get so easy."

Finally the leader of the session is able to stand up and asks the group for some advice. First, introduce yourself and declare your own worst bad habit (the temptation hardest for you to overcome), then offer some advice to those others who have spoken.

Is It All in the Genes?

Most people know their mother, father, aunts, uncles, and grandparents. Many know their great-grandparents as well. A few are lucky enough to have met their great-great-grandparents, but beyond that, it's pretty rare. Today the rage seems to be genealogical digging. Many people spend much of their evenings and yearly vacations tracing their heritage through records at libraries and hospitals all across the country. Some even go to other continents. The point is that either we know our family (physical) roots . . . or we want to know.

That's great, but too often we neglect tracing and remembering our roots in other developmental areas. Here's an interesting twist on "The Family Tree" for you to fill in (as much as you can), tracking your spiritual heritage.

First, find all your pastors' names, and the names of their churches that you attended. Get the dates they pastored that church and the dates you attended those churches, too, if you can.

Pastor _____ of the _____

from _____ to _____.

Pastor _____ of the _____

from _____ to _____.

Pastor _____ of the _____

from _____ to _____.

Pastor _____ of the _____

from _____ to _____.

Pastor _____ of the _____

from _____ to _____.

Now do the same for your Sunday School teachers.

Mr./Mrs. _____ who taught my

_____ class in _____.

Mr./Mrs. _____ who taught my

_____ class in _____.

Mr./Mrs. _____ who taught my

_____ class in _____.

Mr./Mrs. _____ who taught my
_____ class in _____.
Mr./Mrs. _____ who taught my
_____ class in _____.

Now, finally, trace your conversion heritage.

The person who led me to Jesus was _____ in _____
(year). The person who led him/her to Jesus was _____
in _____. And the person who led him/her to Jesus was _____
in _____. And the person who led him/her to Jesus was _____
in _____.

Now cut this out and paste it to the inside cover of your Bible to keep up to date and pass on to your children (someday—not tomorrow).

Christianity: The Alternative Lifestyle

STUDY SCRIPTURE: Matthew 4:12—5:16

KEY VERSE: "At once they left their nets and followed him" (Matthew 4:20).

PERSONAL DISCOVERY

1. OVERVIEW

This passage contains Jesus' first discourse, as related by Matthew. It has come to be known as the Sermon on the Mount or the Great Sermon. Its first section, the Beatitudes, is as well-known a passage from the new covenant as any other. Its other truths offer 20th-century Christians a road map to the lifestyle of righteousness and holiness.

Read these few fact-packed verses, then answer the following questions:

- What is the first thing that comes to your mind when you hear the following phrases?

Fisher of men—

Sermon on the mount—

The Beatitudes—

Salt of the earth—

Light of the world—

- Which beatitude is the hardest for you to understand?

- Which beatitude is the hardest for people to live out?

- What do you see as a common thread between the two episodes with the fishermen (4:18-20; 4:21-22)?

2. DROP 'EM (4:12-22)

This section contains three distinct relocations, first of Jesus himself, then of two sets of brothers. After you read these 11 verses, respond to the following questions:

- Why did Jesus leave Nazareth and go to live in Capernaum?

- Andrew and Simon (Peter) were brothers, as were John and James. Why do you suppose Jesus called two sets of brothers to be His first four disciples?

- What do you think is the significance of these men's occupation?

- What was their response? Did they whine and try to reason with Jesus? Did they suggest they needed to go pray about it? Did they even go tell their families? How would you have responded to Jesus' request?

3. NOW HERE'S SOME GOOD NEWS (4:23-25)

One of the attributes of Jesus that even the world noted and continues to respond to is His healing power. Jesus seemed to have all power over suffering, and when word got around, He was followed by people afflicted with a wide variety of illnesses.

These three verses summarize a lifetime of compassion. Read them, then answer the following:

- If you could ask Jesus today for physical healing for yourself, what one thing would you want Him to heal?

- What societal ill do you pray Jesus would heal today?

- How does the healing ministry of Jesus reflect the essence of the kingdom of heaven?

- Many nonreligious people turn to God for help when they face a crisis. Why do you suppose it takes a sense of desperation for so many to turn to Him for help?

4. THE BE-ATTITUDES (5:1-12)

Like the 23rd psalm and the Lord's Prayer, the Beatitudes are some of the most beloved and memorized verses in the entire Bible. Challenge yourself to commit them to memory in the next few days, then answer the following questions about them:

- How do you "translate" the word "blessed" as it appears in these verses? Does it mean "happy"? Does it mean more than just being happy and carefree?

- The poor in spirit have the kingdom of heaven, while the meek will inherit the earth. Are those two characteristics similar or the same? Are the two rewards similar or the same? The persecuted also receive the kingdom of heaven—how does that fit in here?

- Blessed is not really how most people feel when they are insulted, persecuted, and lied about. How do most people feel? How do you feel?

- There are nine beatitudes. Do the Matthean thing: put them into three groups of three and justify your arrangement.

5. PASS THE SALT, PLEASE (5:13-16)

Jesus ends the introduction to His great sermon with a couple of metaphors: salt and light. After you read these four verses, answer the following questions:

- What is salt used for today? What has been its uses historically?

- If salt that has lost its saltiness cannot be made salty again, does Jesus mean that if we lose our salvation, we cannot be reclaimed?

- Many of us grew up singing "This little light of mine, I'm gonna let it shine." What exactly does it mean to let your light shine? How does one keep it from shining?

- Jesus tells us to let others see our good deeds (v. 16), but later in His sermon (6:1-18) He says that if we pray, or fast, or do any holy thing to impress people, we are simply whistling in the wind. What's the difference?

DISCOVERY GROUP

STUDY SCRIPTURE: Matthew 4:12—5:16

KEY VERSE: Matthew 4:20

Life with an Attitude

Choose a lifestyle in our society and write your own set of "Be-Attitudes." Try nine of them; and you can start off with "Blessed are the . . . for they . . ." Some suggestions might be football (or any sport), school (including students, teachers, principal, etc.), church (including pastor, musicians, board, etc.), children (including sons, daughters, infants, teenagers, etc.), or any other thing you can think of.

Blessed are the

Blessed are the

Blessed are the

Blessed are the

Blessed are the

Blessed are the

Blessed are the

Blessed are the

Blessed are the

Funny, but I Don't Feel So Blessed

On the chart below, write down your "natural" (or immediate) reaction to the following insults, lies, persecutions, and so forth, then fill in your "Christlike" attitude.

The Problem	Natural Reaction	Christlike Attitude
Somebody tells your boyfriend or girlfriend that he or she saw you with someone else last night. (You were really at home the entire evening.)		
The guy next to you in lab is cheating off your test, but the teacher doesn't see it. You do. And the guy gets a higher score than you.		

The Problem	Natural Reaction	Christlike Attitude
Your parents ground you for coming home two hours after curfew, even though you told them the cops stopped you wrongly because your car fit a criminal description.		
You're minding your own business in line at the local burger joint and, out of nowhere, some bully punches you in the back of the head.		
Your boyfriend or girlfriend breaks up with you because of your bad attitude.		

It's Time to Make a Decision

If life is anything, it's making decisions—some of them quickly, some of them after careful thought, some of them down the road a few miles.

The following table offers some examples for you to play with, then asks you to come up with two or three other decisions that might be unique to you and where you are in life. Weigh the pros and cons of each decision to help you finally decide.

Quick Decisions	Pros	Cons
Run the red light		
Homework or TV		
Argue or keep quiet		
_____		
_____		
_____		

Not So Quick Decisions	Pros	Cons
Change jobs		
Buy a new or used car		
Listen to heavy metal music		
_____		
_____		
_____		

Way Down the Road Decisions	Pros	Cons
College or job		
College major		
Single or married		
_____		
_____		
_____		

Shakers and Flashers

Your youth pastor has flipped out! Utterly! Totally! His newest idea is to start two kinds of ministries at your church, and he's appointed you to be on the steering committee to get these things rolling. Really, it's a good idea (you think), but you're completely bamboozled by the names: Shakers and Flashers.

He got this brainstorm, of course, when he reread Matthew 5:13-16, where Jesus tells us we are the "salt of the earth" and the "light of the world." Oh, now you get it—salt*shakers* and *flash*lights.

Here's what he wants you to do: First, come up with a list of ministry ideas for each of the groups. What will the Shakers do and what will the Flashers do? (No overcoats, please!) After you have done that, he'd like to see some of your ideas on designing a sweatshirt for each group—you know, to give them a sense of identity (and to raise some youth group funds—always thinking, this guy).

The Shakers' Ministries

_____

_____

_____

_____

_____

Design their sweatshirt here:

The Flashers' Ministries

_____

_____

_____

_____

_____

Design their sweatshirt here:

3

The Law of Love

STUDY SCRIPTURE: Matthew 5:17—6:24

KEY VERSES: "You have heard that it was said, 'Love your neighbor and hate your enemy.' But I tell you: Love your enemies and pray for those who persecute you." (Matthew 5:43-44).

PERSONAL DISCOVERY

1. OVERVIEW

Now that we have studied what has been called the Preamble to the Christian Constitution, we look next at Jesus' contrasts to Jewish traditional law. As He declared in the opening to this section, however, He did not "come to abolish the Law or the Prophets," but He had come "to fulfill them." Here again is the refrain of Matthew: Jesus is the fulfillment of all Old Testament literature.

Read over these verses carefully and thoughtfully, for they are rich in behavior modification for the Christian. After you have studied them, answer the following questions:

- What do you think is the primary difference between the old covenant (Old Testament) and the new covenant?

- What do you think is the most troublesome verse or verses in this section of the sermon?

- What question(s) do you have that you would like to ask when you meet with your group?

- Is there anything in this passage that seems particularly appropriate for the modern-day reader?

2. INNOCENT OF MURDER? (5:17-42)

This section of the discourse begins with Jesus denying that He was simply the change-agent some of His detractors said He was. His purpose was not just to take away centuries of good laws and grand commandments. His purpose was completion, fulfillment, consummation. He lived on earth to bring sense to the Law, not to make it nonsense.

The next group of verses defines murder as a spiritual act—not merely a physical act. This takes the weapon out of the hands and puts it into the heart, and, as we have learned, the heart is the focus of Christ's ministry.

Read this passage prayerfully, then answer the following questions:

- Define "righteousness" in your own words:

Now define "holiness":

What similarities do you see?

- Jesus views what many believe to be the most serious crime, murder, as a motive of the heart. That makes external appearance superficial, at best, and comparatively meaningless. We can appear virtuous, but if we have hatred in our hearts for someone, we are no better than murderers. Respond to that idea.

- How does Jesus' view of murder differ from that in our society?

- "Raca" is the Aramaic word for "empty-head." (Jesus probably spoke Aramaic most of the time.) That sounds a lot like "airhead," doesn't it? Do you think if you call someone an airhead you are answerable to the Sanhedrin (the church board, if you will)?

- Jesus says that as long as we have turmoil or distrust among us, there is no meaning behind offerings. Why is that?

- President Jimmy Carter got lots of unwanted publicity during his presidential campaign, in 1976, for admitting he had lusted. Jesus clearly calls lust an act of adultery. What do you think is the difference between lust and appreciation for physical attractiveness?

- Divorce is now so commonplace that we don't hear much about it from pulpits. Jesus mentions it from His pulpit (vv. 31-32) and says that only infidelity justifies divorce. Compare this with Mark 10:2-9; what differences and similarities do you see? What reasons have you heard or read about for people today getting a divorce? Do you think those are justifiable? Are those reasons morally Christian?

- Verses 38-42 are pretty tough for most of us to swallow, for they suggest that mercy is the heart of the Lord; therefore, mercy should be the heart of people who call themselves followers of the Lord. Read Exodus 21:23-25. How do you interpret Jesus' interpretation of the Law?

3. TWO SIDES OF THE SAME COIN (5:43—6:4)

Love and hate are more closely related than you might think. If you think in terms of extremes on a straight line, you might put love at one end of the continuum and hate on the opposite end. However, life's situations show us that true hatred is most powerful when directed at someone we have once loved.

Jesus reminds us in this passage that we are not to *be* enemies, even though we will probably *have* enemies. He declares that it is virtually impossible to hate someone for whom you are praying sincerely and fervently. If you lift that name to the throne, God's love will transcend your hatred. (It must have been interesting for Matthew, a reformed tax collector, to hear his profession used as the example for the lowest of the lowlifes when it comes to this "love your enemies" stuff.)

Read over these verses, and then answer some questions:

● How does *love* match up with *giving,* and *hate* match up with *taking?*

● Where in your life is hating your enemies easier than loving them?

● If Jesus were running the government of your country, what changes do you think He would make right away?

● The first four verses of chapter 6 tell us to keep secret our giving and our loving. We aren't to impress others with our compassion, after all; that reward is too temporary even to consider. How do you balance this teaching with the one in 5:16 to "let [our] light shine before men"?

4. THE PERFECT PRAYER (6:5-15)

Have you ever heard someone pray out loud? Of course you have. Have you ever been asked to pray in front of a group? Probably so. Do you pray when you're alone? Good for you.

- What are some of the differences between these three prayers just described?

Jesus saw that even the religious leaders had difficulty understanding the purpose of prayer. They had begun to pray simply for the praise from their listeners: "Oh, Rabbi Sheinstein, that was such a lovely prayer. Your words were beautiful. Will you come to our next party and say a prayer so that all my friends will hear such wonderful words?"

Sickening, but true. And if we were all honest, we do get a little nervous when we have to pray aloud in front of people we don't know so well. We treat our public prayers like some kind of campaign speech. Jesus didn't find that sincere. In fact, He condemned it straight out in verse 5.

Read over these verses, then answer the following questions:

- Why do we get stressed out when we pray in public?

- This sixth chapter to this point is divided into "giving," "praise giving," and "forgiving." How do those ideas merge together?

- This is how Eugene Peterson paraphrases the great prayer (in *The Message*):
  > "Our Father in heaven,
  > Reveal who you are.
  > Set the world right;
  > Do what's best—
  >   as above, so below.
  > Keep us alive with three square meals.
  > Keep us forgiven with you and forgiving others.
  > Keep us safe from ourselves and the Devil.
  > You're in charge!
  > You can do anything You want!
  > You're ablaze in beauty!
  > Yes. Yes. Yes."

What do you think of Peterson's version?

It seems far easier to say "I forgive you" than it is to forget what you did to me. (Of course, we can never erase an experience from our memories. "Forget" here means that we don't allow the past to prevent a healthy relationship with someone in the present and future.) Jesus says you can't have it both ways. Either you forgive others for what they have done to you and don't let that hinder your further relationship, or your Heavenly Father will not forgive and forget what you have done to Him and others.

There are four "fors" to mercy: forgiving, forgetting, forebearing, and foretelling. The first two are rather self-explanatory. The third, forebearing, is patience—certainly a defining characteristic of mercy. Foretelling means just what Jesus said in verses 14 and 15: The level of mercy you extend to others now foretells what will be done to you at judgment.

- What makes the "forgetting" part of forgiveness so difficult for human beings?

- Why is forgetting so imperative?

5. FASTING IS MORE THAN A FAD DIET (6:16-24)

Fasting is never just a physical act—it is a spiritual act. This is quite a consistent sermon, isn't it? Jesus suspects that too often we have gone on prayerful fasts but have forgotten the prayerful part in a hurry. Instead, we focus on how our body is changing, and we begin to seek congratulations from those around us for being holy and righteous.

It's like Franz Kafka's short story "The Hunger Artist," the tale of a man whose occupation is depriving himself of food. His agent books him at carnivals, and for days (his record is 40) he starves himself. Soon the crowds dwindle out of boredom, and Hunger Artist is forced out of a job.

Read over these verses and answer the following questions:

- How do hypocrites fast?

- Have you ever fasted? For how long? For what reason?

- Fasting is a lot like the custom of giving something up for Lent. What does it mean to sacrifice something we love for something we love more?

- Verses 19-24 talk about treasures. Not like the lottery jackpot—in fact, quite the opposite. The treasures that last are immaterial—they can't be held or worn or driven or flown. What are the treasures Jesus is talking about in this passage?

- How would the national economy of your country change if these verses formed the basis of our desires?

- Why is greed such a dangerous sin?

DISCOVERY GROUP

STUDY SCRIPTURE: Matthew 5:17—6:24

KEY VERSES: Matthew 5:43-44

Book 'em, Danno. Murder One.

You've been thrown into spiritual prison for committing murder. You didn't wear a hockey mask and wield a hefty ax. No. Far worse. You wore the mask of a Christian and wielded a hateful tongue. As part of your sentence, you are required to write a letter not only asking forgiveness from your victim but also granting forgiveness for the wrong done to you that triggered such a damning response.

This sentence is not as far-fetched as it first appears. Perhaps you have bad-mouthed someone recently because of some bitter motive, and you do, indeed, need to ask for forgiveness. At the same time, you should forgive and forget. Take this opportunity to do so. (No brownie points for using real names here. Save that for the private letter.)

Dear _____,

Lust Busters

The values clarification class at Valley High School is discussing love today. What a lovely day it is, too, to discuss love. It's one of those spring days young people dream about after a long winter of gray skies and indoor lighting.

Mr. J is a cool teacher who likes to have discussions every Friday, so today they're prepared to discuss. Who doesn't love some babe or hunk, anyway? Let's see what they're saying.

Max: Sure, I feel love for somebody. Shirley is her name, but she doesn't go to school here. I met her at a ball game a couple of months ago.

Mr. J: What do you love about Shirley, Max?

Max: Well, if you saw her, you wouldn't have to ask that, Mr. J. She is F-I-N-E! Capital F. Capital I. Capital N. Capital E. Mmmmm, mmmmm, mmmMMM!

Tena: You're not in love, Max baby. You's in lust!

Max: What do you mean "in lust"? We haven't had sex at all, and we've been out a dozen times. Don't be talkin' to me about lust.

Tena: Yeah, well, all you talked about was how drop-dead gorgeous she is. That's so typically male, man.

Mr. J: Now, Tena, let's be fair. We haven't given Max much time to tell us other things about Shirley, have we?

Justin: But she is F-I-N-E, Mr. J. I seen her. She is one hot woman!

Tena: There it is again.

Mr. J: Let's talk about this for a minute. Who can tell us the difference between these three words: *like, love,* and *lust?* Anybody?

Justin: Yeah, I can. "I . . . like . . . love to lust, man."

Mr. J: You're missing the point, Justin, though I do appreciate the syntax. Seriously, now, who can talk about those three words?

Tony: Try this out. You wanna get into somebody's head—that's "like." You wanna get into somebody's heart—that's "love." But if you just wanna get into somebody's bedroom—that's "lust."

Mr. J: Thanks, Tony. Anybody else?

Heather: I think you like someone who likes you back, but true love, that agape kind of love, loves somebody no matter what they do to you. Lust is simply wanting somebody to do something for you.

Mr. J: Somebody told me once that if you glance at somebody who's great looking and think, "Whoa, he (or she) is good-looking!" you're admiring that person. That's healthy and natural. But if you stare and start letting your fantasies take you into that person's bedroom, then you're walking on thin ice. The first look is OK. The second one may be wrong. The third one definitely *is* wrong.

1. Who do you agree with most?

2. Who would most of the kids in your high school agree with?

3. Who would most of the people in your church agree with?

4. What do you think is the difference between like, love, and lust?

Your Lord's Prayer

Jesus prayed the original prayer in Aramaic, and Matthew wrote it down in Greek. King James had the Greek translated into 17th-century English, and Eugene Peterson brought it into 1993. In your most honest natural language (the way you would talk to your best friend or your favorite sister or brother), paraphrase this short model prayer found in 6:9-13.

Hearts Afire

You think our newspapers are full of bad news? Take a look at Matthew 5 and 6. If we think our prisons are overcrowded today, we ought to study what God finds criminal.

Divide your group into four teams. (Even one person could be a team.) Each team should explore one of these passages:

1. Matthew 5:21-26
2. Matthew 5:27-32
3. Matthew 5:33-42
4. Matthew 5:43—6:4

As you study the passages together, answer these questions:

What does God look at as much as action?

What are Jesus' instructions?

How do Jesus' words fulfill (complete) the Law?

How can we apply His teachings to us today?

What would happen if the government judged its citizens in this way?

Go Ahead, Ask Me; Make My Day

STUDY SCRIPTURE: Matthew 6:25—7:29

KEY VERSE: "Ask and it will be given to you; seek and you will find; knock and the door will be opened to you" (Matthew 7:7).

PERSONAL DISCOVERY

1. OVERVIEW

In our first two studies of the Sermon on the Mount, we have learned what it means to *be* a Christian—what to think and what to do. Somehow, this seems more than a sermon, certainly more than a job description; it's almost like an owner's manual.

The last section of Jesus' discourse concludes with six great lessons for life . . . for survival. As you study these lessons, attempt to apply each one to your life, no one else's. How can each instruction help you, personally, to be a Christian?

Jesus knew the human heart very well. Notice how His lesson about greed—focusing on the material wealth of the world—is followed by a lesson about worry. He knew that contentment in life, whether it be in your job, with your "stuff," or about your relationships, is the greatest antidote to fretting. After all, if your car is a $500 mode of transportation that gets you safely from point *A* to point *B* (even though it looks like it fell off of Gilligan's Island), you tend not to worry about it. But, park a $30,000 vehicle on your driveway, and you can't buy enough insurance, security alarms, and The Clubs. You will lie awake at night, wondering how on earth you can manage the payments.

Jesus also knew that people tend to avoid responsibility for their mistakes and blame other people or forces. "If I had only . . ." or "You know, if she weren't such a . . ." are phrases we mutter all the time. So Jesus not only instructs us to stop worrying about the temporary, earthly stuff but also tells us to cut out the judgmental attitudes we tote around all day long. Instead of kicking others when they're down, we should take a look at our own lives . . . but not overdo that either.

Instead, lean on Him. It's very simple, isn't it? Lean on Him. Rather than over-analyzing your problems or blaming others, go to Him as if He were a loving parent. Watch a child who has a loving home. If things start to unravel as she's playing outside with friends, she runs home to the welcoming embrace of her mom or dad. If the stress of a broken relationship gets to him, he dashes to his comfort spot, home. Jesus reminds all of us that we have a loving Heavenly Father who will greet us in the same way.

Like all good sermons, this one concludes with three illustrations. Jesus loved metaphors (as you know by now), and He used them to give His listeners three insights into the kingdom of heaven. As you study each one, try to write down its meaning in your own words. That will help you understand it better.

After reading this grand conclusion to this great sermon, answer the following:

- What do you think the concluding three metaphors mean?

  The Gates

  The Trees

  The Builders

- What is Jesus' attitude about people in these verses?

- Is there a verse or a point that bothers or maybe confuses you?

- Ask Jesus a question about this passage.

2. A PENNY FOR YOUR THOUGHTS (6:25-34)

Verse 25 of chapter 6 starts off with what grammarians (whoever they are) call a conjunctive adverb. This is a connecting word that links one part of the sentence to a follow-up part. Even though this word begins a new verse and sentence (and in some Bible versions, an entirely new section), it belongs to what precedes it as much as to what follows it. The word is "therefore." (So let's find out what it's "there for!")

The word "therefore" connects the "treasures in heaven" ideal to the "do not worry" lesson. Jesus seems to be saying that if we put all our marbles into one basket, the one we carry around on earth, we're gonna lose all our marbles.

Read through this section carefully and deliberately, and then answer the following questions:

● What three things does Jesus say to stop worrying about?

● What three things do you tend to worry about?

● What three things does your best friend worry about?

● Instead of worrying about those things, what does Jesus instruct us to do?

3. JUDGE NOT! (7:1-6)

Well, now He's really starting to meddle, isn't He? What does He mean, "Do not judge, or you too will be judged"? Talk about taking away some of our funnest fun! That's how we get even. That's how we knock folks down to size.

Aha! That's the problem. We knock them down to *our* size, and Jesus wants us to be "bigger" than that. We need not search the world for scapegoats for our problems. Jesus has already provided one: himself. To place another human being in that position is not only harmful, it's downright sacrilegious!

Read this passage once, then read it a second time. You might even want to do it aloud. Then honestly address the following:

- What is so wrong about judging?

- What people (groups or individuals) do you know who get judged a lot? Maybe even by you?

- What do you think Jesus knew about human nature, about the future, that His listeners (both then and now) didn't (or don't) seem to grasp?

- That dogs and pigs thing in verse 6 is weird. What do you think it means?

4. ASK, SEEK, KNOCK (7:7-12)

Interesting, isn't it, that when you take the first letter of each imperative verb in verse 7 you have the acronym A.S.K. That's not how it worked out in the Greek, but in the English it's almost a pun.

More than clever language, though, this section may be the most important of the entire discourse. It draws a parallel between our Heavenly Father and a good earthly father. It ends in verse 12 with a synopsis of the entire Old Testament (the Law and the Prophets): "So in everything, do to others what you would have them do to you." We know this as the Golden Rule. Ponder these verses, then answer the following questions:

- How can modern-day readers read verses 7 and 8 without thinking they have a magic genie in a bottle?

- What do verses 9 through 11 tell you about the nature of God?

- Write a "for instance" illustration from your own life that demonstrates the Golden Rule.

- Read Luke's version of this same section in Luke 11:9-13. Anything different? Why do you think that's so?

5. THREE KODAK MOMENTS (7:13-29)

Jesus used stories as ancient "photographs" to illustrate His teachings in a memorable form that could be called to mind over and over again. He ends the Sermon on the Mount with three such photographs: the gates, the trees, and the builders. Study each one separately, then view them together and answer the following questions:

- Why do you suppose He called the gate to destruction "wide" and the gate to life "narrow"?

- What is the fruit of the "good tree"? What is the fruit of the "bad tree"?

- You are in the time of life when most Christians wonder, "What is God's will for my life?" That question gets more and more important as you get older. The will of God is a mysterious thing with many interpretations, but it wouldn't be bad to consider verses 24-27 as a capsule explanation of His will. What is He asking you to do?

DISCOVERY GROUP

STUDY SCRIPTURE: Matthew 6:25—7:29

KEY VERSE: Matthew 7:7

Career Day

Mrs. Rowland has been named career counselor for your Bible study group, and it is her job to advise each person toward a career choice. She begins her session with a story about herself.

"When I was just a little older than you are—I had just graduated from college, to be honest—I didn't know what I wanted to do for a living. You know, to make money and survive. It was then that I got some great advice from the twin sister of one of my roommates.

"She told me to make a list of the three things I most wanted to do in my life, so I did. That wasn't hard—I'd been dreaming about these things for a long time: (1) a rock and roll star, (2) a stand-up comic, (3) an editor of a small-town newspaper.

"'Now,' Louise told me, 'go after those things, knowing that God made you and filled you with gifts, talents, and desires, and He's not in the business of tricking people. He won't ask you to do something you hate, are afraid of, or will fail at. That's not His style. So go for it!'

"And did you know," Mrs. Rowland concluded, "I am doing all three of those things today? Sure, it says on my job title that I'm a college professor, but that's not all I do. Once a year I participate in a campus variety show, often singing some golden oldie rock and roll song. Every day I have two or three or four captive audiences in a classroom, who have to listen to my jokes as I teach. And, wouldn't you know it, I'm also adviser of the school paper, so I get to write, edit, and assign stories right along with our student editor.

"Louise was right. And she was right for you too. So what I'd like for you to do right now is to write down the three things you really would like to spend your life doing. Be honest, and be careful. Look at what happened to me."

1.

2.

3.

"Now you may or may not want to prioritize these, but you ought to talk now with your group about what steps you can begin taking to pursue those goals. Don't be afraid. God made you and will never trick you in this decision. Remember, His will is simply for you to build your house on the Rock. He has given you the freedom to decide how to earn the bricks and lumber."

After you have finished, find out from the other people in your group what dreams they have. Do any of them seem outrageous? Do any seem so obvious you wonder why you didn't think of them?

Worrywarts

You've been meeting with these same friends for over a year now at the Angst Café, and every time you get together, you end up talking about the things that are getting on your nerves, stressing you out, keeping you up at night. It's depressing, but for some reason you keep going back; as they say, misery loves company. Let's listen in to some of the conversation over Cokes.

Frettin' Freddy: I don't know what I'm gonna do about my car, guys. It's fallin' apart. The left headlight is out, the front tires are thin, and there's this funny sound when I go past 70 mph. I'd love to just trade it in on a Wrangler or a Mustang, but I can't afford that. That's funny. I can't even afford to get my old car fixed. And the senior trip is coming up, and I'm gonna be stuck on the bus with the rest of the geeks on campus. What a way to go out, huh?

Ann Xiety: Freddy, Freddy, Freddy. When are you going to learn? At least you'll find some kind of solution to your minuscule problem in the next century or two. How'd you like to be stuck with this hair for the rest of your life? Look at it! It's frizzed, fried, and falling out in clumps, and every day it seems to get worse and worse. The doctor says it's stress. STRESS! Now, how's that for irony. The very thing I stress out about is caused by stress. Is that a vicious circle, or what? I'm either gonna have to move to a deserted island, tie my hair up into one of those stupid "do-rags," or fall in love with a balding blind man or a blindingly bald man. Does anyone even know a balding blind man?

Insomni Mac: I do, Ann, but he's married already. My dad is going blind from diabetes. He jokes about it and says that at least he won't have to watch himself get old in the mirror anymore. I'm afraid he's gonna lose his job if he gets any worse. And he tells us that it is gonna get worse. I've been hearing him and my mom arguing in their bedroom at night. I can't tell what they're arguing about, but I can hear them, so I know their voices are getting up there. I'm afraid for my dad, but I'm afraid for Mom, too, because her job is a dead-end job that basically puts food on the table. That's it. Dad could get disability or workman's comp or something, I guess, but what's he gonna do around the house all day long? I'm worried about the whole stinkin' family!

I. M. Stressed: Yeah, my folks fight a lot, too, which just makes my brother, Buzz, stay out even later with his pals, gettin' into stuff I don't even want to know about. I do know Dad's had to go down to the jail a couple of nights to get him, but I don't know what for. His door is always locked—ALWAYS—so I figure he's probably doin' drugs or somethin' stupid like that. Now he's been kicked out of school for a year, which makes me feel even worse about my good grades and bein' on the yell squad. I need to get outta there and get to college, away from it all, but I don't know if I can last that long. It's really bad.

Sam Inex: College. Now there's a hot spot at my house. My parents want me to go to the university because it's close, cheap, and Uncle Fred teaches there, but I really want to go to the church college on our educational zone. I visited there once and really liked the campus and the kids I met, and they have this really great lab for premed. I want to be a doctor, you know. It'd be so great to go there, but the tuition is a billion times more than the state university, and Dad says I'll have to pay for the difference if I go. I've been looking into scholarships, loans, and grants, and that looks pretty good, so I guess I'll be in debt for the rest of my life. Maybe when I finally am a doctor I'll earn enough to pay it off.

Frettin' Freddy: You'll be rollin' in it, Sam. Then you can buy me a new car.

Ann Xiety: Maybe you could specialize in psychiatric care and help all of us deal with stress. Huh?

You: (What's on your mind today?)

Once you have read and completed this dialogue, jot down some things you might say to each of the characters about the way they are dealing with the problems in their lives. Maybe your study group could write its own dialogue from real life.

Here Come de Judge

The People's Court is now in session. Judge Roy Bean is now presiding. Several trials will be occurring today, and you'll be passing judgment on many different people.

Judge Bean is deaf, however, so he has asked each juror to write down his or her judgment so that he can read them all before he hands down his ruling and doles out appropriate sentences.

Murderers—
Child molesters—
Liars—
School cheaters—
Procrastinators—
Old drivers—
Hovering parents—
Homosexuals—
Unwed teenaged parents—
Back stabbers—
Flag burners—
Incompetent employees—
Hypocrites—
Gamblers—
Divorced people—

After you have written your own views on each matter above, go back and play the role of Jesus. How would He rule? Are your judgments different from, or the same as, His? In all cases? What makes the difference in His view and yours?

Fruitcakes

Look around the room you're in right now. Notice each person who is sitting there with you. Make a mental image of those who are absent.

Jesus tells us that we shall know the tree by the fruit it bears. That makes each one of us a fruit bearing tree.

1. List the members of your group below, including your leader and yourself. By each person's name, identify the fruit that falls at the base of his or her trunk.

2. Name the type of tree of each person.

3. How do you know that person's fruit? Was there anyone whose fruit you were unable to identify? Why do you suppose that is? Have you encouraged any of your group lately in the bearing of his or her fruit? When was the last time you bore fruit?

It's a Miracle

STUDY SCRIPTURE: Matthew 8:1—9:38

KEY VERSE: "When Jesus heard this, he was astonished and said to those following him, 'I tell you the truth, I have not found anyone in Israel with such great faith'" (Matthew 8:10).

PERSONAL DISCOVERY

1. OVERVIEW

Jesus walked toward the Sermon on the Mount doing miracles, and, as chapter 8 describes, He left the mountain performing more miracles of healing. It's rather amusing, really, that the people who heard the Master's discourse were so amazed at His authoritative teaching—just wait until they see Him heal the leper and the centurion's servant.

Read these inspiring stories of despair-turned-into-hope, then answer the following questions:

- What do these verses tell you about Jesus that you may not have thought about before?

- Were any of the verses particularly difficult for you to understand?

- How do you define "miracle"?

- If you had followed Jesus off the mountain and seen these mighty works, what question would you ask Him?

2. FAITH FEEDS MIRACLES (8:1-22)

One of the truths that these awesome stories reveal is that faith and miracles are virtually inseparable. Jesus was moved by faith to stop, listen, and allow God's power to flow through Him into the sick and helpless. That certainly is not to say that when the miracle for which we are longing and praying does not happen just as we had hoped it would, we have not exercised enough faith. That is narrow and shortsighted thinking.

Read the first 22 verses of chapter 8, then answer the following questions:

- You will see in the healing of the leper an interesting command from Jesus to this man. What does He tell the man, and why do you think He did that?

- The second miracle is intriguing, in that it features a military man voicing compassion for one of his servants. The word "centurion" means he commanded 100 soldiers, yet he was concerned about a single servant. (Kinda reminds us of the lost sheep story Matthew includes later, doesn't it?) Why is Jesus equally impressed with this man?

- What do you think "demon-possessed" in verse 16 means?

- Jesus seems almost callous in verses 18-22, particularly the last verse. Why do you think He said, "Let the dead bury their own dead"?

3. SEVERE THUNDERSTORM WARNING (8:23—9:13)

Have you ever been out on a boat when a storm hit? The waves can seem like monstrous fists pounding your boat like a sledgehammer. Storms are scary enough when you're on land—inside your house even; how much more alarming when you're being tossed 30 feet into the air over deep water.

The miracle of calming the stormy seas commands our attention because we, too, will face out-of-control situations that place us in grave peril. We need to know that Jesus has been there before, protecting and defending.

Read these stories of miraculous salvation and healing, then answer the questions that follow:

- What was Jesus' purpose in calming the storm?

- What things make this miracle different from those before and after it?

- Jesus seems to honor the request of the demons in the story found in verses 28-34. Why do you suppose He did? And why pigs?

- The healing of the paralytic was an overt sign of power. Jesus was proving a point. Just what was His point?

- We end this section of Matthew with the story of his own calling to become a disciple. What's the most interesting feature of that story?

4. "IF I ONLY TOUCH HIS CLOAK" (9:14-26)

Jesus is grilled by the disciples of John the Baptist about fasting. "Why us," they ask, "and not them?" Read Jesus' response and the accounts of two more miracles, then answer the following:

- Explain the best way you know how about the new wine in old wineskins. Is Jesus referring to the Passover meal before His death?

- Why would the disciples of John ask such a question in the first place?

- The sick woman in verses 20-22 demonstrates remarkable faith in Christ's power. What action in this story makes it different from other miracle stories we have just read?

- For the first time in Matthew's record, Jesus shows His power over death itself (vv. 23-26). Is this a foreshadow of anything?

5. LORD OF THE HARVEST (9:27-38)

Here are three more specific miracles of healing: two blind men and a mute man. By now, the Pharisees are watching Jesus like hawks, trying to catch Him breaking their law so that they might arrest Him and do away with His threat to their power.

Read the verses, then answer the following:

- On what basis, according to Jesus, do these two blind men receive their sight?

- What is the reaction of the Pharisees after Jesus heals the mute man?

- When you read verses 35-38, do you sense that Jesus was frustrated by the enormity of His task? Or was He simply forecasting His short time left?

- The last two verses, 37-38, sound an awful lot like the Great Commission (Matthew 28:18-20). What similarities do you see?

DISCOVERY GROUP

STUDY SCRIPTURE: Matthew 8:1—9:38

KEY VERSE: Matthew 8:10

Turn On the Power

Obviously, Jesus possessed supernatural powers over disease, over demons, even over death. One of the fulfillments of Old Testament prophecy is that the Messiah would have such powers. Look up the following scriptures from the Old Testament and write down what they say:

1 Samuel 10:10 and 11:6

2 Chronicles 32:7

Isaiah 29:18-19

Isaiah 35:5-6

Isaiah 40:10

Isaiah 61:1

Isaiah 63:12

Jeremiah 10:6

Hosea 13:14

What kind of power were these references speaking about? How does Jesus, the Messiah, either contradict, redefine, or fulfill these?

Jesus Christ and the Miracles

No, this is not the name of a new musical group out of Motown, though it is kinda catchy. This section of Matthew lays out a whole series of fantastic and extraordinary stories that show us the tremendous power of the Son of God. (And why shouldn't He have that kind of power? He's God, for cryin' out loud.)

Trace all the miracles that are specifically mentioned in these two chapters and write them down here in the order of their appearance. Next, describe the type of miracle each one is. Then, using a system of 1 to 10, rate the unbelievability factor of each, 10 being the most remarkable miracle you can imagine.

Miracle	Reference	Type of Miracle	Rating

Step Right Up—Who Needs a Miracle?

Make a list below of 10 people you know who need a miracle. Some of them will be personal acquaintances, some of them will be people you have only heard about or read about. After each person's name, describe the situation that placed this person on your list. Then describe specifically what kind of a miracle needs to happen for this person. If you're having trouble getting started, put yourself first. Then your brother or sister. Then your best friend.

Name	Situation	Describe Miracle
1.		
2.		
3.		
4.		
5.		

6.

7.

8.

9.

10.

Now look back over your list. What characteristics in the lives of those you included do you see recurring? Is there one kind of miracle that appears more often than any other?

Place the three most urgent miracles and people on your current prayer list and begin praying for such miracles to take place.

Need a Faith Lift?

Faith, as we know from reading Hebrews 11, is the hope of things we cannot touch or feel, the promise of things we cannot see. Using this definition, we exercise a little bit of faith every day . . . lots of little bits of faith. For instance, we have faith that the sun will come up and go down every day. We have faith that our school will be standing, our friends will show up, and we will eventually pass algebra. We have faith that we will have something to eat today and that the whole family will return home tonight.

In the chart below, list five things under each heading that you have faith will take place. And if you want to test your faith a little bit, make one of them a "fleece"; that is, a hope of faith (a miracle?) for which you are or will be praying. You might begin each one with something like, "I trust that . . ." or "I honestly believe that . . ." or "I have faith that . . ."

Home	Church	School	Relationships	Your Future

Check Your Burdens at the Door

STUDY SCRIPTURE: Matthew 10:1—12:50

KEY VERSES: "Come to me, all you who are weary and burdened, and I will give you rest. Take my yoke upon you and learn from me, for I am gentle and humble in heart, and you will find rest for your souls. For my yoke is easy and my burden is light" (Matthew 11:28-30).

PERSONAL DISCOVERY

1. OVERVIEW

In chapters 10, 11, and 12 of Matthew, Jesus offers His disciples their first commission and identifies himself as the Messiah to them and to John the Baptist. At the same time, Jesus continues to be opposed by the religious establishment. After they see Him driving out evil spirits and demons, the Pharisees suspect Jesus of being aligned with Beelzebub, a ruler of demons.

Read chapters 10—12 and then answer the following questions:

- This passage contains fewer miracle stories and more of Jesus' teachings. Which of His lessons seems most personally directed toward you?

- Which lesson of Jesus is the most difficult for you to understand?

- In His commissioning and sending out of the Twelve (chapter 10), Jesus offers several warnings. Which one seems the most applicable to the 1990s?

- What's your overriding emotion as you complete this passage?

2. WHAT A JOB DESCRIPTION! (10:1-42)

The 10th chapter of Matthew is a powerful, "thick," exciting chapter. Jesus gives the first 12 disciples specific instructions about what He expects them to do and accomplish when He is no longer with them to show them.

As you read this passage, you must say to yourself, "Information Overload! Information Overload!" While it may have sounded overwhelming to mere mortals, it must have also been exhilarating to realize that God was among them, living and breathing right next to them. Can you imagine the thrill of waking up each morning next to the Son of the Creator?

We often call Matthew 28:20 the Great Commission, but it is actually the second of two commissions in Matthew. Chapter 10 contains Jesus' first commission to His disciples. After you have studied it, ponder the following items and write down what you think:

- Jesus uses four animals in verse 10 to illustrate His point. List each one here and write down the meaning that each symbol suggests to you.
  1.

  2.

  3.

  4.

- Jesus called 12 men to be His disciples; Matthew lists them in 10:2-4. Write their names down here. If you know anything about each one of them, write it down. If you don't, write down a question you'd like to ask him directly.
  1.

  2.

3.

4.

5.

6.

7.

8.

9.

10.

11.

12.

- Jesus has been called the Prince of Peace, because He was seen to fulfill the prophecy of Isaiah 9:6. However, in Matthew 10:34, He seems to defy that description. What do you make of that?

- Verse 37 is a tough pill to swallow. Read it in the context of what Jesus has been saying (Luke 14:26 develops it further) and write down what you think He meant.

3. WOE TO YOU (11:1-30)

This chapter begins with a description of Jesus' earthly ministry in which He modeled what we have heard a million times—"Practice what you preach," or more recently, "Walk the talk." That is precisely what the Master was telling those people around Him—and He was not only describing His own ministry but also directing the lifestyle to them.

When the followers of the Baptist ask Jesus in verse 3, "Are you the one who was to come, or should we expect someone else?" He simply tells them (vv. 4-5), "Go back and report to John what you hear and see: The blind receive sight, the lame walk, those who have leprosy are cured, the deaf hear, the dead are raised, and the good news is preached to the poor." That's 5 to 1 in favor of "things seen" over "things heard." A blowout!

Jesus condemns entire cities in verses 20-24, saying, "Woe to you." Peterson says, "Doom to you."

- Why do you suppose Jesus said that?

Read the entire chapter now, and answer all of the following questions:

- What is the exact context in which Jesus invites His followers to rest (vv. 25-30)?

- When in your own life do you find great comfort and solace in that invitation?

- Jesus was to use children to illustrate many things—the kingdom of God, the immature Christian, the deaf audiences. In verses 16-19, He uses children to illustrate something—what is it? Do you find it clear?

4. REMEMBER THIS SABBATH (12:1-21)

Most of us remember the fourth commandment from Exodus 20:8: "Remember the Sabbath day by keeping it holy." The trouble seemed to be in Jesus' day, however, that holiness and the Law seemed to get thrown into the same pot. The scribes and Pharisees turned God's command into their own little words, and then they had the audacity to force their narrow interpretations onto everyone else.

Read about this and the rest of the passage in chapter 12, then answer the following:

- Are there other things in the Bible that you see government or the Church trying to "legislate" today?

- What does it mean to keep the Sabbath day holy?

- How would you define "holiness"?

- Here again we see the letter of the Law being upheld by man over the spirit of the Law (vv. 1-13). Do you find that in other places in Scripture? How about right now in your country?

5. STICKS AND STONES (12:22-50)

This must have been very scary for Jesus' critics, for in these verses we see Him reading their minds. He knows what they're up to, and He lets them have it with both barrels.

They have accused Him of being in consort with the devil. They were afraid that they might be wrong about Him, so they tried to convince everyone that He was wrong about them. Isn't that all too typical of people who are wrong and know they are wrong but are too proud or frightened to admit it?

In verse 37, Jesus makes words very important. You've heard little kids sing out when someone calls them a bad name, "Sticks and stones may break my bones, but words can never hurt me." (What they don't know, right?) Well, Jesus answers that: "For by your words you will be acquitted, and by your words you will be condemned."

Read the last half of chapter 12, then answer the following questions:

- What does Jesus mean in verse 25 when He says that a kingdom divided against itself will be ruined?

- Did you know that Abraham Lincoln quoted this verse in his second inaugural speech? What was the context?

- You've heard it said, "If you're not part of the solution, then you're part of the problem." Jesus says it a bit differently in verse 30. What does it mean?

- The tongue can be our bitterest enemy (vv. 34-37). Why is that?

DISCOVERY GROUP

STUDY SCRIPTURE: Matthew 10:1—12:50

KEY VERSES: Matthew 11:28-30

Legislate This!

Big government is getting more involved in our daily lives, and many other institutions do the same. One example of this is the attempt to legislate morality that seems to consume so many groups today. The following is a list of some of these social issues that are being discussed, both in the political arena and from church pulpits. For each one, write down what government says, what religion says, and then what you say.

Issue	Senate Podium	Church Pulpit	Your Soapbox
Prayer in schools			
Abortion			
Censorship			
Violent crime			
Pornography			
Racism			
Sex education			
Welfare			
Gun control			
Divorce			
Artificial insemination			
Flag burning			

After you have filled in the chart, write down two or three other issues from the national or local television news, from a newsmagazine, or from the newspaper that you can take to your study group for discussion.

_____

_____

_____

Keeping It Holy

Imagine that you've been named to a church committee that is going to make a list of dos and don'ts for keeping the Sabbath day holy, which your congregation is to follow. Your pastor has given you a few suggestions to consider, but she'd like for you to come up with some of your own as well.

Fill in the chart below, placing each of the following items under one of the headings (and write down any conditions that may have entered into your decision). Then add to the chart some items that your pastor may have omitted.

Eating out in a restaurant

Working in the yard

Homework

Watching sports on television

Reading the newspaper

Going to the mall

Going to a movie

Playing an organized sport

Napping

Getting your cat down from a tree (See Matthew 12:11-12 if you snickered at this one.)

Do	Don't

A Rose by Any Other Name

You have a formal Christian name followed by a formal given surname. (That's first and last name, if you want to know.) If you're lucky, you know what your Christian name means. If you don't, you ought to find out (from the dictionary, a Bible dictionary, or a specific name book at your local library).

But you most likely have other nicknames, or pet names, by which you are known or called. Take a moment right now and jot down these "labels" that people have given you. Next to each one, write down the person(s) who call(s) you that name. And if you know how you got that name, write that down too.

_____

_____

_____

Jesus also was known by many more names than the one Joseph and Mary gave to Him. Next to each one below, write down what you know about that name: who called Him that, what that name means, etc. (You may want or need to use your concordance for this.)

Master

Messiah

Emmanuel

Christ

Savior

Teacher

Son of God

Son of Man

Sinner

Blasphemer

Lamb of God

You're Yoking, Right?

Every day at school you eat lunch with the same group of friends. You know them so well that they are open and honest about the stuff going on around them. Oh sure, you spend most of your lunch laughing so hard you can barely eat, but you also spend lots of time in the evenings talking to them on the phone. You know they are "weary and burdened."

First, there's **Matt.** He is good-looking, smart, and athletic, but he's also under a lot of pressure to excel at everything. Some of it comes from his parents, some of it from his family's reputation in the community, and some of it comes from his teachers and coaches. But most of it comes from himself. He kicks himself if he doesn't get 100 percent on every test. He screams if he misses a free throw. He nearly cries if he loses a game of Pictionary or Trivial Pursuit. He doesn't have a whole lot of close friends.

Then there's **Lanya.** No getting around it (almost literally), Lanya is fat. Not just plump or chubby or "filled out." She is as fat as fat is, and she's always been that way. Well, let's be honest—she's 5'1" and weighs over 200 pounds. Her dad is also huge, and her mother wears oversized dresses. Face it—they're a fat family. Lanya has one best friend and lots of friendly faces around her, one of which is yours, but none of the boys talk to her. She'll be graduating next spring, and she's never been on a date.

And what about **Bruce?** Bruce comes from a loving family, hard workers, but they don't have a lot of money. They live in a very small house in the poor part of town. Bruce shares a room with his little (as in two-year-old) brother. There's just nowhere else for little Tommy to sleep. Bruce's clothes are old-fashioned but meticulously clean, and his hair is on the shabby side. His grandpa cuts it. Oh yeah, that's another thing—Bruce's grandpa lives with them too. He sleeps on the Hide-A-Bed in the living room. Bruce sees you and others at school and wonders why he has to be so poor when others who are good people and really nice to him seem to have everything they want.

Finally, there's **Monique.** She's the only Black person in the entire school. She is also one of the most outgoing and positive people you know. She is on the cheerleading team, is sophomore class vice president, and gets pretty decent grades in her classes. Her parents are divorced, and her older brother is a member of a local gang. He's been in trouble with the law quite a bit lately. She calls you at least once a week to see how you're doing, and despite what you know is difficult at home, she's always happy. Or at least she seems to be.

Some of these kids seem to "have it all together," but some are obviously suffering in one way or another. We've all got burdens. As best you can, try to come up with at least one wearisome burden for each of these "friends of yours," then write down what "rest" or relief they would find with Jesus.

After doing this for these four fictional friends, do the same thing for four real friends you have.

Friend's Name	*Burden*	*"Rest"*
Matt		
Lanya		
Bruce		
Monique		
1.		
2.		
3.		
4.		

7

The Parables

STUDY SCRIPTURE: Matthew 13:1-58

KEY VERSE: "Have you understood all these things?" (Matthew 13:51).

PERSONAL DISCOVERY

1. OVERVIEW

Do you like stories? Well, do you? Then you're gonna love chapter 13, because it's full of them, seven to be exact. Jesus liked stories, too, and He used them frequently to explain what life in the Kingdom is like, both in His day and now, centuries later.

We call Jesus' stories parables, that means "a placing aside" from the Greek *parabolē.* You might be more familiar with the word *illustration,* which means virtually the same thing. A parable applies concrete imagery and detail to an abstract idea. It makes the idea come alive so that we can understand it better.

As you read and study chapter 13, watch for the details in each story that help you grasp the truth Jesus was trying to communicate. Then answer the following questions:

- The disciples ask Jesus why He's telling them stories when there seem to be so many other more important things to say and do. What is His response to their question? (see vv. 10-17).

Take a quick inventory of the parables in chapter 13. Give a title to each one to complete the phrase, "The Parable of the _____."

_____

_____

_____

_____

_____

_____

_____

What binds each one together? What are they all describing?

- Which parable was the most confusing to you?

- What question would you like to ask the Master Storyteller?

2. A TIME TO HARVEST (13:1-23)

This parable illustrates the urgency of spreading the gospel of Christ and salvation. It also explains the difference between the wise listener and the foolish one, who refuses to heed the warnings. After you finish reading this section of chapter 13, answer the following:

- First read the parable (vv. 3-9), then read Jesus' explanation (vv. 19-23). Write down the explanation of each of the symbols He uses in the story.
  The birds—
  The farmer—
  The seed—
  The rocky soil—
  The thorns—
  The good soil—

- This parable describes four kinds of "soil." Can you think of another kind of soil that might accept or reject the gospel?

3. WHEAT OR WEED? (13:24-30, 36-43)

You may have noticed that the explanation of the parable about the weeds sown among the wheat is interrupted in the text by a third parable, which we will study later. The parable of the wheat and weeds logically flows out of the preceding parable, for it, too, is about seeds and sowing. However, this parable is not so much about the hearers of the gospel as it is about the enemies of the gospel.

As you read this parable, look again at the details Jesus used to illustrate His point. Then look at His explanation and draw some parallels between the symbol and its meaning.

The sower—
The field—
The weeds—
The enemy—
The harvest—
The harvesters—

- Why do you suppose Jesus used the field and the seed to provide the backdrop for His stories?

- Where was Jesus when He told these first two parables in chapter 13?

- How do you think His listeners responded to these two stories?

4. FOUR SNAPSHOTS (13:31-35, 44-46)

These two passages contain four very brief, yet powerfully clear, pictures of the kingdom of heaven. Read them now, then answer the following questions:

- The mustard seed was the smallest seed used by farmers then, but its plant could reach 10 feet in height eventually. What makes that a powerful picture?

- Yeast permeates dough and makes it expand. How is the kingdom of God like yeast?

- Why was the man who found the treasure in the field so happy that he sold everything he owned?

- The merchant does the same thing as the man in the field. What makes this parable different from that other one?

- The final parable uses the sea as the setting—how appropriate for Jesus' fishers of men. Let's analyze its meaning as we did the first two parables, shall we? What do you think the symbols mean?

  The lake—

  The good fish—

  The bad fish—

  The fishermen—

5. YOU CAN'T GO HOME AGAIN (13:53-58)

Jesus realized something on this trip that many adults who have left home, become somewhat successful (or at least renowned), then returned home have discovered. You're always the little boy or girl you were when you lived there.

Think about it: What if Jesus had grown up as a little boy in your neighborhood—nothing outstanding about Him, really. He had gone away for some time, then returned spouting mammoth ideas about who He is and who God is. Wouldn't you wonder a little bit?

Read this passage, then answer the following:

- It says in verse 57 that they took offense at Him. What do you think they said?

- Where is Jesus' hometown?

- Did you know Jesus had brothers? What were their names? Were they also Sons of God?

- He also had sisters. Why aren't they mentioned by individual names, like the brothers? Why was Mary named but not Joseph?

DISCOVERY GROUP

STUDY SCRIPTURE: Matthew 13:1-58

KEY VERSE: Matthew 13:51

The Moral of the Story

Aesop, the Brothers Grimm, Mother Goose, even Dr. Seuss (and others) have all written stories about life for children. Each of these fables carries with it a moral, what might be defined as an overriding truth.

Below, you will find some familiar story titles from your childhood. Next to each one, write down the lesson to be taken from the story. Chances are you won't remember every one equally, and you may find yourselves having to look back at those books. You may need to ask a parent where those books are (and take a flashlight in the attic).

Hansel and Gretel

The Ugly Duckling

Little Red Riding Hood

Goldilocks and the Three Bears

Cinderella

The Three Little Pigs

The Cat in the Hat

Snow White and the Seven Dwarves

Rappunzel

Jack and the Beanstalk

The Kingdom of Heaven

Jesus told seven stories in chapter 13 to describe the kingdom of heaven. Most of us have individual visions of what heaven is like (like John did in Revelation, but not nearly as profound or scary). Some of us picture long, white beaches with crystal blue seas, no sharks, and lots of free time. Others of us imagine ourselves skiing down evergreen-lined slopes at 40 mph until we collapse by the fire and drink hot chocolate. Some envision themselves behind the wheel of a 1998, $200,000, bright red sports car, taking the turns like it's floating on air. Your parents may simply picture a few days with no stereos within 400 light-years.

Whatever you picture heaven being like, write down as many of those visions here as you can think of. (Hint: Think of heaven as a combination of all of your favorite things.)

Heaven

A Personal Parable

You've been asked by the disciples to be a speechwriter for Jesus. Not that He really needs one, but He knows you need to feel needed, so He is asking you to give Him a good illustration for His next sermon.

That sermon will not be about heaven but rather about the Christian life. You may choose any idea in that theme (joy, love, compassion, servanthood, peace, mercy, grace, patience, kindness, etc.) and write a story that illustrates that idea. It might be a true story from your own life, or it might be straight out of your imagination.

Who Are You, God?

You are so excited. After years of hearing about your parents' trying to get on the show, you've just found out in the mail that you have been selected to be a panelist on the new version of that old game show **"To Tell the Truth."**

You fly to Los Angeles in your new clothes, ride in the limo to the Hollywood studio, and soon find yourself sitting on a panel with Dick Clark, Markie Mark, Oprah Winfrey, and Paul Shaeffer. This is UNBELIEVABLE.

Suddenly the curtain lifts, revealing three contestants, two of which are impostors. The host, Bill Murray, opens by saying, "Ladies and Gentlemen. Seated in front of you are three men, each claiming to be God. Your job is to find out which one is telling the truth. Contestants, take your turn and convince these people you are God."

Contestant No. 1: You should be very afraid of Me. I'm watching you every day like a hawk, and I can't wait to catch you doing wrong, thinking something bad, or saying something nasty, so I can punish you. I love to make rules and watch you trying not to break them. Rules, rules, rules. I love them. I've got a ledger up here—one side for bad things and one side for good things. I hardly ever write anything on the good things side. When you fill the bad things side, I'm going to zap you and you will spend forever in fire. You might put on a good front, but I know how evil your thoughts are, and this bad side is filling up fast.

Contestant No. 2: I'm not the bad guy that this fellow has described. I'm just a little insecure, I guess. I want for you to succeed and to do well in all that you do. Yes, I sure do. After all, I made you, and I would be stupid if I didn't want the best for you. However, I do expect some thanks now and then. Maybe a bunch of money in the offering plate, maybe 15 percent tithe, maybe a loud prayer in front of a lot of people. I surely want you to read the Bible every minute you can, because if you don't, it makes Me feel like you don't love Me much.

Contestant No. 3: I am the Creator of all that is, was, or will be. I made the earth you stand on, the water you drink, and the sky you look into. I made the animals in the jungle, on the plains, in the air, and in the seas. And then I decided to make you. You are My supreme creation, such a marvelous being. I love you more than anything else I have made or ever hope to make. You often get off track, though, I'm sorry to say, but I provided a way to get you back safely. That way cost Me the life of My only Son, but you were worth it. I rescued Him too, and now He lives with Me today.

The host says, "Panelists, it is your turn to ask one question, then you'll have to vote."

Write your question here:

Now vote:

Walking on Water

STUDY SCRIPTURE: Matthew 14:1—15:39

KEY VERSE: "But Jesus immediately said to them: 'Take courage! It is I. Don't be afraid'" (Matthew 14:27).

PERSONAL DISCOVERY

1. OVERVIEW

Matthew recorded a number of Jesus' miracles in the first 13 chapters of his Gospel. The miracles recorded in chapters 14 and 15 are three of the best-known in the entire new covenant: feeding more than 5,000 people with five loaves of bread and two fish; walking across stormy waters to meet His disciples; feeding more than 4,000 more hungry mouths with seven loaves and a few fish.

Talk about awe inspiring! Talk about extraordinary! Talk about frightening! Jesus was all about those things. He was also about understanding and love.

Read these two chapters and answer the following questions:

- Which of these three miracles impresses you the most? Why?

- How would you have reacted if you had seen your teacher walking across the nearest lake?

- In these chapters, which of Jesus' sayings is the most difficult for you to understand?

- What prayer would you write here before you begin digging into this passage?

2. LET'S EAT (14:1-21)

This passage contains the stories of two feasts—one an orgy of sensual pleasure and decadence, the other a miracle of loving provision and intervention.

As you read about these two instances, contrast their details and their meanings, then answer the following:

- Who was at the first feast (vv. 1-12)?

- Who was at the second feast (vv. 13-20)?

- Why was Herod afraid of John the Baptist?

- Jesus seems to be so calm during what we might consider crises, doesn't He? Here, He's been healing the sick all day long. The disciples suggest that Jesus send the crowds of needy people away so they can eat. He simply asks what the disciples have to eat so that the crowds can stay a while longer. What does His calm response tell you about Him?

3. STORM SURFING (14:22-36)

As soon as the disciples had collected all the leftovers from the miraculous feast—about 12 boxes full—Jesus told them to leave and get some rest, sending them off in a boat. He decided to stay behind for a while. Read the details of this famous miracle, then answer the following:

- What did Jesus do after the disciples left in the boat?

- While they were sailing across the water, they soon encountered resistance. They were going one way, but the wind and the waves were knocking them back the other way. In what ways might this image be a symbol of the Christian experience?

- What great words of comfort does Jesus give His men? What crisis are you going through today for which those words might be fitting?

- What is Peter's response to seeing Christ?

- Why did Peter start to go under?

- When everybody was safe in the boat, the disciples recognized something. What did they say? Why was this sign so revealing to them?

4. DON'T LET YOUR WORDS BECOME AIR POLLUTION (15:1-20)

After feeding the masses, walking on water, and healing more sick people, Jesus is once again attacked by the Pharisees, who are still bent on finding fault with what He is doing. They set out to trick Him at His own "game."

Read this exchange and answer the following:

- What are the Pharisees asking Jesus all about? What is their sole (soul) motive?

- Jesus rebukes them, calling them a name (v. 7). What does that label mean?

- As Jesus often does, He quotes from the Scriptures, the Word of His Father, to answer hostile inquiries. Here He quotes from Isaiah. In your own words, what is He saying?

- If you could apply to your own life and your own situation what Jesus says about being "unclean," about what goes into a person and what comes out of a person, how would you make that application?

5. IT'S A DOG-EAT-DOG WORLD (15:21-39)

Faith seems to be a key element in Matthew's Gospel. This passage begins with the emotional pleas of a Canaanite woman for "crumbs" from the Master's side, and ends with collecting seven basketfuls of "crumbs." As you read, consider the following questions:

- Why are the disciples seemingly so dense? Just a few days earlier, hours perhaps, they had claimed, "This is it—the Guy is truly the Son of God!" Now they're telling Him to send this screaming woman away. Are they being selfish, or protective?

- The screaming woman wants Jesus to exorcise the demons in her daughter, and He says something very interesting: "It is not right to take the children's bread and toss it to their dogs." Does your Bible explain that? If not, what do you think it means?

- The second miraculous feeding story has some similarities, of course, to the first, but it is what's different that makes it more interesting to look at. What are some of those distinctions?

- Read about this same story in Mark 7:31—8:10. Do you note any differences in that account of this same feast?

DISCOVERY GROUP

STUDY SCRIPTURE: Matthew 14:1—15:39

KEY VERSE: Matthew 14:27

Pop Quiz

Let's take a few minutes to try our hand at answering the following multiple-choice questions about this passage. Choose the best answer for each question below.

1. Which person shows the most faith in these two chapters?
   A. Peter
   B. The Canaanite woman
   C. The Pharisees
   D. The crowds

2. Which of the following vices that come from the heart do you think is the worst?
   A. Evil arguments
   B. Lies
   C. Cussing
   D. Fornication

3. Who is Jesus most like?
   A. A genie in a bottle
   B. A faith healer
   C. A Supreme Court justice
   D. An emergency room doctor

4. What does Jesus think about the Pharisees?
   A. "Give me a break!"
   B. "They'll come around. Give 'em time."
   C. "They're the worst sinners of all."
   D. "If this is the Church, I want no part of it."

5. Which word best describes the heart of the Lord?
   A. Mercy
   B. Justice
   C. Judgment
   D. Patience

Are You Hungry?

Think back over the past two weeks. How many times have you eaten each of the following foods?

___ Pizza

___ French fries

___ Tacos

___ Salad

___ Fried chicken

___ Burgers

___ Milk shakes

___ Green vegetables

___ Baked potato

___ Steak

Now you can plan your favorite meals. Place a check mark next to each item you want for breakfast, for lunch, and for dinner. If the item is followed by parenthetical choices, circle one of those.

Breakfast

___ Eggs (scrambled, fried, poached)

___ Sausage (links, patties)

___ Hash browns (shredded, diced)

___ Cereal (What kind? _____)

___ French toast

___ Pancakes

___ Waffles

___ Juice (orange, grapefruit, grape, apple)

___ Milk

___ Coffee

Lunch

___ Pizza (What kind? _____)

___ Burger and fries

___ Hot dog/corn dog

___ Fried chicken

___ Roast beef

___ Salad

___ Fried fish

___ Tacos

___ Coke

___ Dr. Pepper

___ Lemon-lime

___ Cherry Coke

___ Root beer

Dinner

___ Soup (What kind? _____)

___ Salad (Caesar, fruit, tossed green, Jell-O)

___ Bread (French, rolls, wheat, white)

___ Potatoes (baked, mashed, scalloped, fried)

___ Vegetables (peas, beans, broccoli, cauliflower, carrots, mixed)

___ Meat (steak, roast beef, grilled chicken, stuffed pork chops, fish fillets, hamburger, baked ham)

___ Pasta (spaghetti, fettuccine, lasagna, manicotti)

___ Dessert (cookies, pie, cake, ice cream)

Bonus Points

If you'd like, describe the setting and company you would have for any or all of the meals you've chosen above.

Atti-foods

Which of the following statements best describes your attitudes about food and eating?

____ "I think about eating all the time. It seems I'm always hungry."

____ "Ach. Food. I can take it or leave it."

____ "I like how it tastes, but I'm always watching my weight, so it's kind of a curse."

____ "My parents make a bigger deal about what I eat than I wish they would."

____ "Eating is a time to get together with family or with my friends. What food I actually eat is secondary."

____ "There are some foods I just am plain afraid to eat. I'm afraid they'll make me throw up."

____ "If people would let me, I'd live on one thing: _____."

____ "Food is so expensive. I feel guilty when I eat too much."

____ "The world hunger problem gets to me whenever I sit in front of a big meal."

____ "I eat three square meals a day."

Unclean and Clean

Read the words of Jesus as they are paraphrased by Eugene Peterson in *The Message:* "Listen . . . It's not what you swallow that pollutes your life, but what you vomit up. . . . Don't you know that anything that is swallowed works its way through the intestines and is finally defecated. But what comes out of the mouth gets its start in the heart. It's from the heart that we vomit up evil arguments, murders, adulteries, fornications, thefts, lies, and cussing. That's what pollutes" (vv. 10-20).

First, offer your feelings and thoughts on the following things that come out of the mouth. You might even rank them from worst to least bad.

Cussing

Lying

Gossip

Criticism

Arguing/bickering

Second, you know that the Church does have standards of behavior for its members. Some of them you may agree with wholeheartedly; some others you may question. What is *your* personal stance on the following issues, keeping in mind that "What goes into a man's mouth [read "heart"] does not make him 'unclean,' but what comes out of his mouth [heart], that is what makes him 'unclean'" (15:11).

Dancing

Movies

Drinking alcohol

Working on Sunday

Smoking

Other issues

9

Signs! Signs! Everywhere Are Signs!

STUDY SCRIPTURE: Matthew 16:1—18:35

KEY VERSE: "I will give you the keys of the kingdom of heaven; whatever you bind on earth will be bound in heaven, and whatever you loose on earth will be loosed in heaven" (Matthew 16:19).

PERSONAL DISCOVERY

1. OVERVIEW

At first glance, you may think these three chapters of Matthew are just like the ones you've already read. You find a little bit of instruction, a few miracles, some parables, a little bit of divine frustration. And in a way, you'd be right, for that is precisely what is included in these chapters.

This surface similarity is a good reason to read each section as if it were all by itself. This is done most easily if you use a Bible that divides the chapters into separate episodes and stories. (The NIV does this well; so does *The Message,* a paraphrase in modern language by Eugene Peterson.) Each story that Matthew tells contains a compelling truth about or insight into God's kingdom.

Because this is a fairly long section of Matthew, allow enough time to read it slowly, perhaps in several settings. Ponder each division without being hurried to the next. Once you have finished reading the entire section, answer these rather general questions:

- What one verse in this section do you think is the most important one?

- Is there a verse or passage that really challenges the way you think or live?

- What question would you like to ask your group leader, or—if you could go back in time—would you have asked Jesus himself?

- If you had been one of the 12 disciples present at these events, what would you be thinking about now?

2. THE MARK OF THE YEAST (16:1-28)

This chapter opens with another "stupid" request from the hypocritical cynics who plagued Jesus' ministry. The narrative then heads into more revelation as to the nature of God and His Son, the Messiah, and Jesus—first from himself, then from Peter, the Rock. The chapter concludes with Jesus' prediction of His arrest and death. As you read each of these four stories, concentrate on the following questions:

- Look at 12:39-40, and any notes your Bible might include, to discover what Jesus meant by "the sign of the prophet Jonah." What is the sign?

- What is the "yeast" Jesus warns His disciples about in verses 5-12?

- The keys mentioned in our Key Verse (get it?) are alluded to in Acts 2. Read that story, concentrating on Peter's role, until you get an idea of what these "keys" are, then write down your findings here.

- Matthew 16:21 marks a second change in the focus of Jesus' ministry (the first was in 4:17). Look at the verb "began." What was He beginning?

3. THE SUMMIT MEETING (17:1-23)

Most Bible versions call the first 13 verses of chapter 17 "The Transfiguration," because it includes visages of Elijah and Moses, making this one of the biggest spiritual summit meetings that have ever taken place. (And some folks think a Beatles reunion would be a big deal!) If that weren't enough to make it one of the most memorable days in the lives of the disciples, who else should show up but God himself. No wonder they wanted to erect monuments. Instead, Jesus wants them to keep it hush-hush.

- Why do you think Jesus is so insistent that no word gets out about this summit meeting?

- Why do Peter, James, and John get to see this? Is there something special about those three?

- Why do you suppose Peter suggests the three shelters (monuments, really) idea?

- Was it Elijah there on the mountain, or John the Baptist?

- In verse 20, Jesus once again brings up the mustard seed illustration. Where have you seen that before, and what was its meaning? What does it mean here? Are there any differences?

4. MAY I BE THE GREATEST? (17:24— 18:9)

Jesus performs a minor miracle that may seem to us more like a magic trick. He pulls a coin out of a fish—rather, He has Peter do it. But, as usual, it is to teach us a lesson.

- What do you think that lesson was? What do the kings, their sons, and others mean?

The first nine verses of chapter 18 contain one of the great lessons we need to hear over and over again, especially when we start to get a little pious and proud about our "saintly" behavior. Doesn't it sound just like us to ask, "Hey, Master, who's the greatest in Your kingdom?"

- Who *is* the greatest in His kingdom?

- What is it about children that makes them the greatest in God's eyes?

- What is a millstone?

5. AS WE FORGIVE OUR DEBTORS (18:10-35)

Are there limits to how far God will go to rescue us? Are there limits on what we can ask God to do for us? Are there limits to our forgiveness of others? No. No. No. Read these verses, note the familiar verses you may have heard before, then answer these questions:

- Who is represented by the lost sheep? Who are the 99 other sheep?

- What does Jesus really mean when He says we need to forgive each other 490 (or in some versions 77) times?

- The Sermon on the Mount talks about forgiving someone who sues you. Matthew 18:21-35 also seems to indicate that we are to forgive anyone who owes. Are these two principles practical in this day and age?

DISCOVERY GROUP

STUDY SCRIPTURE: Matthew 16:1—18:35

KEY VERSE: Matthew 16:19

Denying Yourself

Jesus makes himself very clear to Peter at the end of chapter 16: "If anyone would come after me, he must deny himself and take up his cross and follow me" (v. 24). In the chart below, offer as many examples of denying, taking up, and following as you can think of. An example is printed to help start your thinking.

Deny	Take Up	Follow
That great jacket at the mall	$100 saved	Buy jackets for the girls next door

It's Mountain Moving Day

Do you think Jesus was kidding when He said that if we have even the tiniest bit of faith we can command a mountain to move? If you do, then consider this: The mountains Jesus meant were not the Rockies or Mount Rushmore. That would be easier than some of the mountains He was intending. After all, for some of the "mountains" you ask Him to move, He may hand you the shovel.

Here is a brief list of some of the obstacles that you may consider mountainous. Circle those that apply to you, then write down why those "mountains" are in your life, why you want them "moved," and the method (shovel) you might need to consider.

Mountain	Why It's There	Why You Want It Gone	Shovel
Complexion			
Body build			
Hair			
Grades			
Intelligence			
Finances			
Popularity			
Parents			

Car
Teachers
Siblings
Boss
Job

I've Got a Secret

This activity is a private activity that will not be shared with anyone but God. To make sure that happens, you don't even have to write it here, but there is room for you if you'd like to tell God your greatest, deepest secret.

Jesus asked the disciples to keep several events and ideas secret. Reflecting on the passage we read for this lesson and the passages before, what are some of the things Jesus wanted His men to keep under their hats?

Matthew 6:1—

Matthew 6:6—

Matthew 17:9—

Matthew 8:4—

Matthew 9:30—

Mount Rushmore

If you've ever visited the Black Hills of South Dakota, you've probably stood in awe at the sculpture carved into one of those granite hillsides, featuring the likenesses of George Washington, Thomas Jefferson, Abraham Lincoln, and Teddy Roosevelt. In chapter 17, Peter proposed something like a Mount Rushmore for Elijah, Moses, and Jesus. If you were going to construct a Mount Rushmore of the Bible, limiting yourself to four faces each for the Old and New Testaments, who would get on there?

Old Testament

    1.

    2.

    3.

    4.

New Testament

    1.

    2.

    3.

    4.

Now let's have a little bit of fun. Let's broaden the scope to other areas.

Your local church

    1.

    2.

    3.

    4.

Television/movies

    1.

    2.

    3.

    4.

Music (you choose what kind)

    1.

    2.

    3.

    4.

Sports (you choose which one)

    1.

    2.

    3.

    4.

10

Tickets, Please

STUDY SCRIPTURE: Matthew 19:1—20:34

KEY VERSE: "So the last will be first, and the first will be last" (Matthew 20:16).

PERSONAL DISCOVERY

1. OVERVIEW

This is a great passage of information about the kingdom of heaven and how to get there. If you've been a bit perplexed about the sure ticket to heaven, just read chapters 19 and 20—Jesus makes it pretty clear. Once you have finished your reading of this section, answer the following:

- According to Jesus, who will get into heaven?

- How does a person get into heaven?

- What section or verse in this reading bothers you?

- What is the most helpful truth among the many here?

2. JUST DO IT (19:1-15)

The pattern we've become accustomed to in Matthew's account repeats itself here in chapter 19. Jesus has just performed some miracles and is teaching the crowds when the Pharisees show up again.

"Hey, Jesus," they ask, "when can a man divorce his wife without committing a sin?" They were trying to trick Him with one of their legal questions (although it makes you wonder if some of them were looking for a way to escape their own bad marriages). However, in any case, their trick was bound to fail, because they didn't realize that as the Son of God, *Jesus created the Law of Moses!* Note what He says, then answer the following items:

- Jesus referred to Genesis for God's original design for marriage. What is that ideal?

- What is the one exception to staying married?

- That's not the way it is in our day, is it? You can even see commercials on television for $68.00 divorces. Some lawyers make quite a good living handling divorces—not all adulterous ones, either. Our society is full of people who are divorced, many for reasons other than adultery. What do you think Jesus would say to us about the topic of divorce?

- Marriage is not for everybody, according to Jesus (vv. 11-12). What three groups does He mention specifically?

- Jesus then says that if we don't fit into any of those groups, we should go for it. Why do you think He states it so strongly?

3. THREADING THE NEEDLE (19:16-30)

Modern Christians often live a double life that presents ethical dilemmas. On the one hand, our economic system tells us to strive for wealth. On the other hand, our Master tells us to give it all away. Read this passage and see what you come up with in response to these questions:

- How would you personally define success and prosperity?

- What does Jesus tell the rich young man his ticket into the Kingdom is (vv. 17-21)?

- Why does the rich young man turn on a dime and leave so disappointed?

- If you could summarize what Jesus is telling *you* in this story, what would it be?

4. COMING IN LAST (20:1-19)

The last thing Jesus says in the preceding story about the rich young man is, "Many who are first will be last, and many who are last will be first." Glance ahead, if you dare—doesn't He say that very same thing in verse 16 of this chapter? And if you want to see it one more time, He says basically the same thing in verses 26-27. That's three times. Read the first 19 verses of chapter 20, then answer the following questions:

- What exactly does it mean—the first will be last and the last first?

- How many groups of men does the landowner hire, and at what times?

- What does the landowner want these men to do? Where will they be working? How significant is that? (Read John 15 before you answer that last question.)

- How would you have responded if you had been in that first group of employees? How would you have reacted if you had been in the last group hired? What makes the difference in your feelings?

5. SURROUNDING THE THRONE (20:20-34)

Pardon the pun, but it seems ironic that this passage begins with 20:20. (That's the measure of perfect vision, and in this passage Jesus attempts one more time to give His disciples perfect vision of their roles in the Kingdom.)

Unlike Mark's version of this story (he writes in Mark 10:35-37 that James and John themselves asked the question), the mother of the two disciples who had accompanied Jesus up the mountain of transfiguration (the summit meeting He has with Elijah and Moses) asks Jesus if her sons can surround Him when He ascends to the throne.

Note His lengthy response, the other disciples' reaction, and His final entreaty before He heals two rather persistent blind men. Then answer the following questions:

- Why would the Zebedee boys' mother make such a request?

- What does Jesus mean when He forecasts that they indeed will drink from His cup? (Hint: He's not simply talking about the Last Supper Communion cup.)

- Notice that the other disciples get pretty upset with James and John and their request. Why were they so uptight?

- Jesus says one of the greatest lines ever uttered about himself in verse 28. What exactly is He saying about himself and, therefore, us?

DISCOVERY GROUP

STUDY SCRIPTURE: Matthew 19:1—20:34

KEY VERSE: Matthew 20:16

The American Dream

In a recent class meeting of the Ethics and Economics course at the nearby college, the professor led a discussion about the values that separate the Christian view of success from the world's view. Let's hear what some of the students are saying.

Lorna: I'm so sick and tired of people getting on the case of those who have earned a respectable place in life. My mom and dad work really hard in their jobs—my mom's a lawyer and my dad's a doctor—and we have just about everything we want or need. Is there anything wrong with that? I think God rewards those who work hard. Besides, we're some of the biggest contributors to our church. I'd even go so far as to say that if we pulled out our tithe checks, that place would fold in a month.

Jeff: I tend to agree with that, Lorna, except it seems you might be a little too proud of your church support. My hope is that one day I can earn $5,000,000 so that I can give $1,000,000 away. That's twice what the Bible says I should give in tithe. I think it'd be so cool to see the face of somebody who's been handed a million bucks, don't you?

Hank: I just want to be comfortable. I'd like to have a car that runs—and one for my wife, if I'm lucky enough to get married before I die—a warm home, not too big but roomy enough so I don't have to step over stuff to get to my bed, lots of friends, and nice clothes to wear to work. Oh, and great dinners. Steaks! I don't need a whole lot of the nice things I see on television, but I don't want to have to worry about paying the bills, either.

Susan: You know, I've heard all of you talking about all that you can get and have and still be Christian. Maybe I'm way off, but when I read about people who have very little, some have nothing, I can barely stand to talk about it . . . or think about it. And it's not just in some third world country, either. There are people in this city who scrounge in garbage cans and sleep in downtown doorways. I want to make sure that happens to one less person because I was on earth. Whatever it takes to do that, that's what I'm gonna do. Anything else I *get* or *have* will be the proverbial icing on the cake.

Sharon: I think our government needs to do more to help those people, Susan. We need more assistance programs to get those people on their feet. Sure it would take more tax dollars in that direction, but we probably have a lot of programs being funded in Washington that don't need to be around anymore.

Doug: Whoa, Sharon, and Susan, and the rest of you bleeding hearts. Those people you describe scrounging in garbage cans are there because they put themselves there. Somewhere along the line they chose to climb off the train to success and take the easy way out, and now they're paying for their laziness. The last thing government needs to do is support these people any more. What we need to do is stop those kinds of welfare programs, because they encourage laziness and promiscuity and the other evils Jesus condemns in His Word.

The discussion will continue for several more minutes, but you tune it out because you've started thinking about what you believe when it comes to money and Christianity. Why don't you write down some of your initial thoughts and reactions to this class discussion? Who's right and wrong? *What* is right and wrong?

It's Your Serve

Your local *Antelope Club* is planning its next service project in the community, and your fellow members have asked you to rate some of the activities they have suggested to the headquarters in Summerhaven City. You are to place a number between 1 and 10 (10 being the most effective—1 being the least effective) next to each. Then, if you have more than one 10 on the chart, rank those in order of importance.

Proposed Project	Rating
Pick up street litter	
Paint address numbers on curbs	
Paint widows' homes	
Serve meals to homebound people	
Hospice services for AIDS patients	
Mow yards for old people in the neighborhood	
Serve meals at the local rescue mission	
Collect old bikes to fix up and give to poor children	
Work at the local convalescent home	
Reading program for the elderly	
Literacy programs (tutoring the illiterate)	
Fund-raisers for the club	
Giant community garage sale	
Pantry for the homeless	
Consignment clothing shop	

For Richer or Poorer

You have your own perceptions of what it means to be rich and what it means to be poor. Whether it's material wealth, relational wealth, or spiritual wealth, you have a pretty good idea of what this means to you.

In the chart below, offer 5 to 10 traits of each. They have examples printed already to get you started:

Materially

Wealthy
Mitsubishi 3000GT
10 room house

Poor
1975 Dodge Dart
Utility apartment

Relationally

Wealthy
A best friend since kindergarten
Loyalty

Poor
I've got real enemies
I feel all alone out there

Spiritually

Wealthy
Jesus calls me by my first name
I'm currently involved in service

Poor
Legalism
I'm too busy for service to another

Fair Is Fair

"Life is not always fair." Has your father or your mother ever said this to you when you've been griping about things not going your way at school or at home? Probably so. Think of as many occasions/situations as you can where you've thought you received a bum deal . . . first at home, then at school.

Home

_____

_____

_____

_____

_____

School

_____

_____

_____

_____

_____

Now take a look at one of the more "painful" entries you've just made and explain the circumstances here. What happened? What should have happened in your opinion?

(Here's the hard part.) What do you think Jesus would advise you to do with this problem you've just described?

11

Hosanna in the Highest!

STUDY SCRIPTURE: Matthew 21:1—25:46

KEY VERSE: "I tell you the truth, whatever you did for one of the least of these brothers of mine, you did for me" (Matthew 25:40).

PERSONAL DISCOVERY

1. OVERVIEW

The week that begins with Jesus' triumphal entry into His beloved city of Jerusalem has often been referred to as *Passion Week*. From the end of this week to His ascension, the story becomes quite familiar: the Last Supper, the betrayal, the arrest, trial, Crucifixion and Resurrection—now that's a full week for us to study. This week is the climax of what God has done for us through Jesus, and Matthew lets us in on the greatest story ever told. Are you ready? Read these chapters (this is a long passage), and then answer the following questions:

- Look up the word *passion* in your dictionary. What does it mean? Try to consider all of its meanings and not just the reference to this week.

- Some thoughts and even some words that Jesus uses in this section of Matthew are repeats from previous passages. What are they?

- What did you read in this section that you hadn't known or thought much about before?

- As you finished reading this section, what would you like to have said to Jesus, had you been there?

2. "THIS TOOK PLACE TO FULFILL . . ." (21:1-46)

It's interesting that this week seems to capsulize the entire life of Christ: the Triumphal Entry, various trials and inquiries, rejection. His patience with human beings, alone, let's us know that He is *different.* As you read His words of instruction and compassion, think about His suffering, His humanity. Then consider the following items:

- Why did He ride a baby donkey into Jerusalem? Doesn't that seem like an odd mode of transportation for a man, much less the Son of Man?

- Jesus enters the Temple (vv. 12-17) and seems to "snap." This section is often used to show His human side, but it is more than just a temper tantrum, isn't it? He is showing us something much more important than that He had a "mean streak." What is it?

- After demonstrating His power and His truth through the withering fig tree, Jesus is once again questioned by the chief priests: "Who gave you this authority?" Don't you know how frustrated He must have been that they insisted on this line of inquiry rather than opening their eyes and *seeing?* How did Jesus respond?

- What do the two parables (vv. 28-32 and 33-46) say to you about the Kingdom?

3. LOVE YOUR NEIGHBOR (22:1-46)

Always the teacher, Jesus continues what He alone knows is His last week by offering pictures of His kingdom and what one must do to inherit it. Instead of running and hiding as any other person would have done (note the disciples' reaction to the hostility later), Jesus keeps trying. Chapter 22 contains more of His parables and more examples of rejection. Read these stories, some of them more familiar than others, and then answer the following questions:

- The wedding banquet parable is as direct as any He has told (vv. 1-14). In your own words, draw as many parallels to the real situation as you can. (Who is represented by the servants? The invited guests? "Anyone you find"? The wedding banquet itself?)

- What does Jesus' response to the question about taxes tell you that you can apply to your own life?

- What does it mean to love your neighbor as yourself? Is that possible without obeying the commandment that precedes it?

- At the end of this chapter it says "From that day on no one dared to ask him any more questions." Why not?

4. WHOA, WOE, AND WOW (23:1—24:51)

If chapter 23 doesn't get your attention with "woe" after "woe" after "woe," you might want to check your pulse. Then in chapter 24 we get His prophecies of the end of the age: the apocalypse. These are fascinating chapters to read, even though a bit difficult to understand. Read them slowly, then respond to the following questions:

- If you had been the target of Jesus' strong words in chapter 23, which of the "woes" might have seemed to be the most frightening and negative?

- Which of His warnings in chapter 24 is the most difficult for you to understand?

- So-called modern prophets have tried to predict the Lord's return for the past 2,000 years, and all of them have been wrong. What does Jesus say about His return (vv. 36-51)?

- Which verse from these two chapters is the one you want most to remember?

5. SHEEP AND GOATS (25:1-46)

In this final bit of instruction to the crowds before He is turned over to His executioners, Jesus offers us three more parables—the 10 virgins, the talents, and the sheep and goats. Read each one and answer the next four questions:

- What is the bottom-line truth of the story about the 10 virgins (vv. 1-13)?

- Did you know "virgins" referred to "bridesmaids"? How does this new information affect your interpretation of the story?

- What does the "talent" represent in the parable of the three servants (vv. 14-30)?

- Verse 40 has one of the great truths of the entire new covenant, particularly as it pertains to compassionate ministry. What does it mean to you?

DISCOVERY GROUP

STUDY SCRIPTURE: Matthew 21:1—25:46

KEY VERSE: Matthew 25:40

Dear Diary

It's a good thing for us that some people wrote down the major events in Jesus' life, but what if He had kept a log of His activities himself?

Try to write a daily journal entry for each of the seven days of Passion Week as Jesus might have recorded it—in the first person. (Notice you'll have to go beyond chapter 25 in order to record Thursday through Sunday, but much of that is pretty familiar to you already.) Don't be too detailed (you don't have a lot of room or time) . . . just the highlights.

Palm Sunday:

Monday:

Tuesday:

Wednesday:

Thursday:

Friday:

Saturday:

Sunday:

This Is How God Showed His Love

Certainly the entire life of Jesus shows us how much God loved us—"that he gave his one and only Son" (John 3:16). Most of Christ's instructions are also reflective of that theme—"This is how God shows His love."

In a brief paragraph (or list of sentences, or even just a bunch of phrases and words), write down at least 5 ways God shows His love for *you*. Some of you may want to write 10. Some may want to write even more.

_____

_____

_____

_____

_____

Now consider how you might pass that around a little bit. If God loves you without condition or reservation, you must love others too. You can't have it just one way. Next to each name below, write down at least one or two ways you will show that person love this week.

Mom—

Dad—

Brother(s)—

Sister(s)—

Teacher—

Neighbor—

Best friend—

A complete stranger—

This Is the Truth

These four chapters contain seven stories, most of which are labeled as parables in your Bibles. Each is listed below with its reference. You should write next to each the truth that it teaches you. Try to make it as personal as you can.

Two sons (21:28-32)—

Tenants (21:33-46)—

Wedding banquet (22:1-14)—

Taxes (22:15-22)—

Ten virgins (25:1-13)—

Talents (25:14-30)—

Sheep and goats (25:31-46)—

EXTRA! EXTRA! Read All About It!

Jesus used what was happening in the Holy Land for the basis of most of His teachings. The funny thing is that those same things are happening today. It's almost as if He was reading today's headlines.

In chapter 24, Jesus mentions several incidents and events that will occur in the last times—those are listed below, along with their references. By referring to current newspapers and newsmagazines, even the television news, write down any headlines that would apply to any of the prophecies from chapter 24.

People claiming to be holy (24:5, 11)

Wars and rumors of wars (24:6)

Famines (24:7)

Earthquakes (24:7)

Martyrdom (24:9)

False signs (24:24)

Natural changes (24:29)

Thirty Pieces of Silver

STUDY SCRIPTURE: Matthew 26:1—27:31

KEY VERSE: "He went away a second time and prayed, 'My Father, if it is not possible for this cup to be taken away unless I drink it, may your will be done'" (Matthew 26:42).

PERSONAL DISCOVERY

1. OVERVIEW

Here it is, Wednesday, the 14th of Nisan (late March/early April), A.D. 30. Jesus has done all that He can do to convince His closest followers, His crowds, and His religious leaders that the kingdom of God is at hand, right here in front of them.

Walking.

Teaching.

Healing.

Touching.

Now it is time for Him to fulfill His single most important mission: Forgiving.

Study these verses carefully. Try to let what is happening come alive—become real. This is suffering and upheaval like few have ever known. Imagine His emotions. Picture His anguish. Absorb His strength and patience. Understand His sacrifice.

- Is there anything new you learned by reading this passage this time?

- Is there anything that happened in the section that you've known about for a long time?

- What question would you like to take to your group study?

- Were you bothered or confused about anything in this passage?

2. THE PAYOFF (26:1-16)

You've heard the adage "When the going gets tough, the tough get going." Now you've read a story in which this saying comes alive. The going is about to get really tough for Jesus, but it is at this point that He stands firm, tall, and strong. As you read about the plot to betray and kill Jesus, consider these questions:

- What was Judas's motive for turning Jesus over to the chief priests?

- Why did the priests want to avoid any trouble during the Passover feast?

- Why did the disciples turn so vehemently against the woman who anointed Christ with perfume?

- Do you think this episode with the woman and the perfume was a fore-shadow of the anointing of His body for burial? Why or why not?

3. THE HOLY COMMUNION (26:17-35)

Known both as the Lord's Supper and the Last Supper, Christ's celebration of the Passover feast (the Feast of Unleavened Bread) transformed the Jewish tradition from a symbolic ritual into a true sacrifice of himself. It's no accident that the Lord's

Supper is called a "sacrament," which comes from the same Latin word that "sacrifice" does. (Bet you already knew that.)

At the end of the meal, Jesus makes a startling prediction that is simply too hard to believe . . . especially for one of the disciples. Read these verses, then answer the following:

- The disciples know things are beginning to unravel for them, but sitting there with the Master, eating and celebrating together, they must have been relatively relaxed. Suddenly He pops up with one of the truly ear-opening statements of all banquets in history. What does He say?

- What is their immediate reaction?

- In that culture, having supper with someone meant "I'm your friend—I will never hurt you." Judas knew that. Does that make his act seem worse?

- Read Exodus 12 and write down the meaning of the original Passover.

4. HANDS UP (26:36-75)

Jesus now does something most of us probably would have done in that situation—He goes to pray. Pray hard! When faced with something horrible or frightening, the first thing we Christians tend to do is cry out (some of us more loudly than others), "WHY ME?"

Read these verses, and then answer these questions:

- In verse 42, Jesus uses the metaphor of the "cup" passing from Him. Does that mean anything significant?

- This whole week is full of threes. There is a set of threes in verses 38-44: Jesus goes away three times to pray. What other threes can you think of or find in this last week of His life?

- Why do you think Jesus calls Judas "Friend"?

- One of the Twelve pulls a sword to defend Jesus, but he is rebuked. What does Jesus tell him?

- The trial is a mockery—both of the truth and of Jesus' divinity. First He remains silent, then when confronted directly with the question, "Are you the Son of God?" Jesus says simply and humbly, "I am." What is the reaction to that?

- How many times does Peter deny Jesus? Next, read John 21 and count how many times Peter affirms his love for Jesus. Does that seem significant for any reason?

5. "GIVE US BARABBAS!" (27:12-31)

By now it is Friday, and Jesus faces one last trial, this one before the political governor, Pilate. Pilate is completely unprepared for what hits him. Jesus is brought before him as a religious prisoner accused of blasphemy, not a capital offense at all. That is why the Jewish leaders try to describe Jesus' Messiahship as a political claim to be "King of the Jews." Read about this trial and Christ's scourging, then answer the following:

- Who is Barabbas? What has he done to get himself thrown on the same platform as Jesus?

- Pilate sees that his only escape is to fall back on a custom that is so little used it is found only in the Gospels (no other historical documents). What is that custom?

- Only Matthew records the incident with Pilate's wife (v. 19). What does she say?

- Do you remember the Beatitudes in chapter 5 of Matthew? Which ones come to mind as you read these verses about the trial and the whipping and the mocking?

DISCOVERY GROUP

STUDY SCRIPTURE: Matthew 26:1—27:31

KEY VERSE: Matthew 26:42

Why Me?

You've been invited to a Pity Party tomorrow night after school at Jessica's. You have to bring one dish of self-pity, but you don't want to bring what everybody else is bringing—you take pride, after all, in being original. You decide to make a few phone calls to find out what others are bringing.

Mark: I'm bringing "Chips on the Shoulder." It's easy, and there's always enough around at my house. My mom hates her job and lets the world know about it when she gets home. "I wish I didn't have to work," she complains. My dad loves his job, so he thinks my mom complains too much. He comes to ask me advice all the time about what he should do. My sister thinks she is the ugliest person on earth. (She is.) I feel like I'm the only one on the planet who doesn't have a car. Yep, that's plenty for Jessica's party.

Marilyn: What to bring? That's a tough one, because I don't know if I'm going to go to the party at all. I was really excited when I heard about it, because I know the people who are going, and it should be one of the pitiest of pity parties ever held, but now I'm depressed about what I should bring. They'll laugh at me, I know, so I don't know what to do. Hey, maybe I'll bring "Dip in Mood."

Blake: I hadn't planned anything for tomorrow night, because I really need some time to myself. I haven't caught up on last semester's homework yet, not to mention last week's; I haven't slept well in so long I can barely walk; I've been running here and there and, frankly, I think I should pull back a little and say no to things for a while. But now I feel so much pressure to go to that party. I just hate spontaneous setbacks like that: I've planned to rest and relax by myself, and I get thrown right back into the fray. Maybe I'll bring Mom's "Surprise Snack."

Jane: I'm taking some "Humble Pie." It's what everybody expects of meek little Jane, now isn't it? Come to the party . . . get laughed at . . . get made fun of . . . get put down. That's our Jane. If one person in this world would appreciate me for one split second of my life, I think I might explode with joy. Nobody at school likes me. My so-called friends at church talk about me behind my back. Even my parents are starting to look at me funny. I may not go to the party at all. I'd just hate to miss it, though.

So now that you've called your friends (with friends like that, you ought to be pitied), you have decided what you'll be bringing to Jessica's party. Write it down here and explain why that seems appropriate for you.

Friends in Low Places

All of us have friends, but sometimes we don't like the way they treat us. Listed below are several of these mistreatments—take a look at them. Next to each one, place a number between 1 and 10 to reflect the severity of pain each causes. Ten means it hurts almost too much to overcome. One means you'll probably forget about it by tomorrow.

Mistreatment
Lying about you
Borrowing something without asking
Cheating off your homework or test
Ditching you at a party or game
Forgetting a date or arranged meeting
Backing out on a commitment to help you
Neglecting to call you for a week
Not believing something you've told him or her
Always asking to borrow money
Rarely repaying debts
Stealing another friend of yours away
Pretending he or she doesn't know you when you've gotten into trouble
Siding with your parents in a disagreement
Ratting on you to some authority
Acting like an idiot when you've been pulled over by the police
Always playing to win at everything, always overly competitive
Following you around everywhere, doing exactly what you do
Doing things intentionally to make your parents mad
Bumming a ride off you all the time
Quitting something you started together, leaving you alone

Ranking
Now look at all the items that received a 10 and rank those to come up with the absolute worst thing that person could do to you. If the worst thing is not on the list, write it here:

What would it take for you to forgive (and forget) this person's offense?

Take It to Court

Maybe you think there's no way you could forgive that person for what he or she did to you. Instead, you think it can only be resolved by taking him or her to court and having a judge and jury decide this person's fate. Here is your chance to do that.

Appoint the most objective and impartial person in your group to be judge. Maybe it will be your group leader. It could be a fellow student. How about your pastor? Next, appoint a defense lawyer, someone who will stand by the accused and defend him or her with whatever means he or she can come up with. You, of course, will be the prosecutor, bringing to the court all the grisly details of the offense.

The rest of your study group can function as the jury—listening and deciding what can be done to atone for such a horrible thing, should they find the person guilty, of course.

The Lord's Supper

As you wrap up this lesson, take a few moments to reflect on the sacrament of Communion, the taking of the elements as representations of the sacrifices made on your behalf by the Messiah, Jesus Christ.

Make it a true Love Feast by using small loaves of hard bread (sourdough hoagy buns work well) and a single chalice of juice. As you share your loaf of bread with the others in the group, tell them each one thing you appreciate about them. Tell them you love them and will pray for them—if you mean it sincerely. Your leader will encourage you to close with prayer for each other.

13

So Send I You

STUDY SCRIPTURE: Matthew 27:32—28:20

KEY VERSES: "Therefore go and make disciples of all nations, baptizing them in the name of the Father and of the Son and of the Holy Spirit, and teaching them to obey everything I have commanded you. And surely I am with you always, to the very end of the age" (Matthew 28:19-20).

PERSONAL DISCOVERY

1. OVERVIEW

Can you believe it? We are nearly at the end of our study, and today's lesson focuses on the last minutes of Christ's earthly life and the first minutes of His heavenly reign. In these verses you'll read how much He loved you. After you have finished, answer the following questions:

- What happens in these verses that you'd like to ask your leader about?

- Which verse supplies you with a much-needed sense of hope?

- What do you think the disciples were thinking before 28:16?

- What single word (this will be hard) capsulizes this section? How about the entire Gospel?

2. ON THE CROSS (27:32-44)

Jesus has reached the point of no return—actually, He had reached this point the day He was born. Now Jesus was nailed to a cross He had been forced to drag through the streets until He collapsed from exhaustion on the outskirts of town. Read these verses, then respond to the following:

- Who was Simon of Cyrene, the man who bore the cross of Jesus after He could carry it no farther?

- How do you suppose Golgotha got its rather descriptive name?

- Does your Bible include any explanation of what "gall" is? If so, write what you think Jesus' refusal to drink it meant. If not, be sure to ask your fellow students what they came up with.

- Neither Mark nor Matthew includes the request of the crucified thief to be remembered by Jesus when He entered His kingdom. For that, read Luke 23:32-43. What does that exchange tell you about Jesus and His kingdom?

3. "ELOI, ELOI, LAMA SABACHTHANI" (27:45-56)

The last three hours of Jesus' life must have seemed eerie and surreal to those standing around the Cross. Although it was only noon, the skies became black. As we read, we see His pain, His courage, and His love. After you have finished this brief section, answer these questions:

- What does "Eloi, Eloi, lama sabachthani" mean? What did those standing nearby think Jesus was saying?

- As soon as Jesus surrendered His Spirit, the curtain that separated common people from the inner courts of the Temple was torn down the middle. What does this symbolize?

- Only Matthew records the mass opening of tombs and the resurrection of holy people (vv. 52-53). What does this scene signify?

- Note what the centurion says in verse 54. Finally he seems to understand who Jesus is. Do you think it takes this kind of event for some to get it? Why might that be?

4. LAID TO REST . . . TEMPORARILY (27:57-66)

After Jesus died, several of His associates, including Mary Magdalene, Mary the mother of James and Joses, and Mary the mother of James and John, came to retrieve His body and give it a proper burial in the borrowed grave of Joseph of Arimathea. After you read this account, answer the following:

- It seems significant that the tomb was borrowed. How does that fact help you to understand what was happening and going to happen?

- The skeptics, cynics, and critics were out in force, scared to death they might be proven wrong by this "dead man." What did they ask Pilate to provide?

- What is the irony in the phrase "made the tomb secure"?

- What was the purpose of the seal on the stone?

5. IT ALL BEGINS (28:1-20)

It had been a dark, dismal Friday and a long fearful Saturday. *But Sunday has come.* This is the single most important day in all of Christian history. Prophecy had been fulfilled. Death had been conquered. Provision had been made for eternal life. Atonement. Redemption. Reconciliation. Salvation. As you complete your study of this great gospel of hope, answer the following:

- Describe the appearance of the angel at the tomb. What happened there?

- Note that Jesus then appeared to the two women who had anointed Him in life, attended Him as He died, cared for His body after He had died, and sat nearby as He lay in the tomb. What does this tell you?

- Jesus calls His disciples "brothers." This is the first time He does this. What does this label mean about their relationship?

- Describe how you feel when reading the last words of Jesus recorded here (vv. 19-20).

DISCOVERY GROUP

STUDY SCRIPTURE: Matthew 27:32—28:20

KEY VERSES: Matthew 28:19-20

Let There Be Hope

Few days go by that you do not utter at least one sentence that begins with "I hope . . ." It may be "I hope he asks me out for Friday night." Or "I hope Mr. Johnson cancels the test today." Or "I hope I don't get in trouble in Mrs. Smith's class today." We also say sentences like that for the coming year: We call them New Year's resolutions. And then there are those hopes that are for a lifetime. Using all three of these ideas, complete the following sentences as honestly as you can.

Everyday hopes

I hope _____

I hope _____

I hope _____

I hope _____

I hope _____

Resolutions for the year

I hope _____

I hope _____

I hope _____

I hope _____

I hope _____

Lifetime hopes

I hope _____

I hope _____

I hope _____

I hope _____

I hope _____

That's News to Me

You're a reporter for the *Golgotha Gazette,* and your editor has sent you to cover the execution of a Galilean Jew named Jesus, whom some have called the Messiah. Like any good cub reporter, you know you have to get the five *W*s and one *H*—Who, What, When, Where, Why, and How. Your editor has put the rush on this story for tonight's edition. See if you can help him out.

Who? _____

What? _____

When? _____

Where? _____

Why? _____

How? _____

Now write the story here. Try to make it sound as much like an objective story as you can. You might even want to read a few stories in your hometown newspaper before starting.

The Funeral That Never Was

Jesus was buried immediately after His death, with no funeral service, no tributes, no eulogies. Assuming there had been one, what things might you have said at such a service? Here are some of the things people share at memorial services. Do your best to write some of the service.

Dates of birth and death:

Hometown:

Family members:

Job title:

Coworkers:

Accomplishments:

Greatest attributes/characteristics:

Things that were important to Him:

Thanks a Lot

One thing we never do enough is thank people for what they do and who they are. Here is a chance for you to write three thank-you notes as you complete this series of studies. You are actually encouraged to send one of them (you'll figure out which one). Spend some time thinking about what you'd like to say before you actually start writing.

To your Discovery Group leader

To Matthew

To Jesus, your Messiah